What is Digital Journalism Studies?

What is Digital Journalism Studies? delves into the technologies, platforms, and audience relations that constitute digital journalism studies' central objects of study, outlining its principal theories, the research methods being developed, its normative underpinnings, and possible futures for the academic field.

The book argues that digital journalism studies is much more than the study of journalism produced, distributed, and consumed with the aid of digital technologies. Rather, the scholarly field of digital journalism studies is built on questions that disrupt much of what previously was taken for granted concerning media, journalism, and public spheres, asking questions like: What is a news organisation? To what degree has news become separated from journalism? What roles do platform companies and emerging technologies play in the production, distribution, and consumption of news and journalism? The book reviews the research into these questions and argues that digital journalism studies constitutes a cross-disciplinary field that does not focus on journalism solely from the traditions of journalism studies, but is open to research from and conversations with related fields.

This is a timely overview of an increasingly prominent field of media studies that will be of particular interest to academics, researchers, and students of journalism and communication.

Steen Steensen is Professor of Journalism and former (2016–2020) Head of the Department of Journalism and Media Studies at Oslo Metropolitan University. He currently leads the international research project *Source Criticism and Mediated Disinformation* (2020–2024). He is associate editor of *Journalism Practice* and has a background as a journalist.

Oscar Westlund (PhD) is Professor in the Department of Journalism and Media Studies at Oslo Metropolitan University, where he leads the *OsloMet Digital Journalism Research Group*. He holds secondary appointments at Volda University College and the University of Gothenburg. He is the editor-in-chief of *Digital Journalism*. He leads *The Epistemologies of Digital News Production* research project funded by the Swedish Foundation for Humanities and Social Sciences.

Disruptions: Studies in Digital Journalism
Series editor: Bob Franklin

Disruptions refers to the radical changes provoked by the affordances of digital technologies that occur at a pace and on a scale that disrupts settled understandings and traditional ways of creating value, interacting and communicating both socially and professionally. The consequences for digital journalism involve far reaching changes to business models, professional practices, roles, ethics, products and even challenges to the accepted definitions and understandings of journalism. For Digital Journalism Studies, the field of academic inquiry which explores and examines digital journalism, disruption results in paradigmatic and tectonic shifts in scholarly concerns. It prompts reconsideration of research methods, theoretical analyses and responses (oppositional and consensual) to such changes, which have been described as being akin to 'a moment of mind-blowing uncertainty'.

Routledge's new book series, *Disruptions: Studies in Digital Journalism*, seeks to capture, examine and analyse these moments of exciting and explosive professional and scholarly innovation which characterize developments in the day-to-day practice of journalism in an age of digital media, and which are articulated in the newly emerging academic discipline of Digital Journalism Studies.

User Comments and Moderation in Digital Journalism
Thomas B. Ksiazek and Nina Springer

Smartphones and the News
Andrew Duffy

What is Digital Journalism Studies?
Steen Steensen and Oscar Westlund

For more information, please visit: www.routledge.com/Disruptions/book-series/DISRUPTDIGJOUR

What is Digital Journalism Studies?

Steen Steensen and Oscar Westlund

Routledge
Taylor & Francis Group
LONDON AND NEW YORK

First published 2021
by Routledge
2 Park Square, Milton Park, Abingdon, Oxon OX14 4RN

and by Routledge
52 Vanderbilt Avenue, New York, NY 10017

Routledge is an imprint of the Taylor & Francis Group, an informa business

© 2021 Steen Steensen and Oscar Westlund

The right of Steen Steensen and Oscar Westlund to be identified as
authors of this work has been asserted by them in accordance with
sections 77 and 78 of the Copyright, Designs and Patents Act 1988.

British Library Cataloguing-in-Publication Data
A catalogue record for this book is available from the British Library

Library of Congress Cataloging-in-Publication Data
Names: Steensen, Steen, (Professor of journalism) author. | Westlund,
    Oscar, author.
Title: What is digital journalism studies? / Steen Steensen, Oscar
    Westlund.
Description: London ; New York : Routledge, 2020. | Includes
    bibliographical references and index.
Identifiers: LCCN 2020019445 | ISBN 9780367200909 (hardcover) |
    ISBN 9780429259555 (ebook)
Subjects: LCSH: Online journalism—Research. | Online journalism—
    Research—Methodology. | Digital media—Research.
Classification: LCC PN4784.O62 S73 2020 | DDC 070.1—dc23
LC record available at https://lccn.loc.gov/2020019445

ISBN: 978-0-367-20090-9 (hbk)
ISBN: 978-0-367-55123-0 (pbk)
ISBN: 978-0-429-25955-5 (ebk)

Typeset in Bembo
by Apex CoVantage, LLC

Visit the eResources: www.routledge.com/9780367200909

Contents

Figures

Tables

Foreword

This book is intended for researchers, PhD students, and possibly also post-graduate students interested in the emerging field of digital journalism studies. The book would not have materialised without the aid of many people, to whom we would like to extend our warmest gratitude. First, we would like to thank series editor Bob Franklin for reaching out to us with the idea for this book. Without his encouragement and enthusiasm the book would not have been written. Then we would like to thank our employer, Oslo Metropolitan University, not only for allowing us to spend time on this book, but also for granting funding for making this book Open Access. We are truly excited about the fact that this book can be accessed by anyone from everywhere without any costs other than those related to having internet access and a screen to read on. We would also like to thank the publisher, Routledge, for making this opportunity available at a reasonable cost, and for all the work put into the production of the book.

In the final stages of developing this book we have approached a handful of exceptionally qualified peers for feedback on one or several chapters. Each chapter has benefited substantially from constructive feedback on both bigger and smaller issues. In alphabetical order we would like to extend our most sincere appreciation and thanks to Laura Ahva, Sherwin Chua, Mark Deuze, Scott Eldridge II, Tine U. Figenschou, Alfred Hermida, Kristy Hess, Avery Holton, Karoline A. Ihlebæk, Maria Konow Lund, Merja Myllylathi, Ragnhild K. Olsen, Chris Peters, Jane B. Singer, Helle Sjøvaag, and Edson Tandoc Jr. We will forever be grateful for your collegial support.

The book is written as a cooperative exercise between the two of us. Even though all eight chapters are coauthored, we have divided the work so that Steensen had the main responsibility for chapters 1, 5, 6, and 7 while Westlund did the heavy lifting in chapters 2, 3, 4, and 8. However, all chapters have been revised by both authors in many rounds, so the

book is really the result of what we have experienced as a fruitful cooperation. Our final acknowledgement therefore goes to ourselves: Steen
would like to thank Oscar and Oscar would like to thank Steen. We have
enjoyed the experience of working with each other and integrating our
explicit knowledge about digital journalism and digital journalism studies
in coauthoring this book. It's been a challenge, but it has been fun.

Oslo,
18-March 2020

1 The introduction

The premises and principles of digital journalism studies

On 11 April 11 2018, Mark Zuckerberg, the Facebook CEO, sat before the US Congress for a hearing following the Cambridge Analytica scandal. He had already survived 10 hours of questioning the previous day. The session chair, Republican congressman Greg Walden, leaned forward in his large, black leather chair, his stare alternating between his paperwork and Zuckerberg, who sat behind a long but modest desk, several feet below him. Walden said:

> Welcome, Mr. Zuckerberg, to the Energy and Commerce Committee in the House. We've called you here today for two reasons. One is to examine the alarming reports regarding breaches of trust between your company, one of the biggest and most powerful in the world, and its users. And the second reason is to widen our lens to larger questions about the fundamental relationship tech companies have with their users.

Walden then laid out in more detail the background for these two concerns, before focusing on the questions he wished Zuckerberg to answer:

> There are critical unanswered questions surrounding Facebook's business model and the entire digital ecosystem regarding online privacy and consumer protection. What exactly is Facebook? Social platform? Data company? Advertising company? A media company? A common carrier in the information age? All of the above? Or something else?

Zuckerberg was not allowed to answer, yet. He sat there quietly behind his desk, occasionally sipping water out of a white paper cup, while looking at Walden like a school boy paying attention to his teacher. It was not until a couple of hours later, following a series of questions from other congress members, that Walden returned to the questions regarding what kind of company Facebook actually is and asked Zuckerberg a direct question: "Is Facebook a media company?"

Zuckerberg did not take his eyes off Walden and answered, with a steady voice:

> Thank you, Mr. Chairman. I consider us to be a technology company, because the primary thing that we do is have engineers who write code and build products and services for other people. There are certainly other things that we do, too. We – we do pay to help produce content. We build enterprise software, although I don't consider us an enterprise software company. We build planes to help connect people, and I don't consider ourselves to be an aerospace company. But, overall, when people ask us if we're a media company, what – what I hear is, "Do we have a responsibility for the content that people share on Facebook?" And I believe the answer to that question is yes.[1]

This answer – in fact the whole Facebook hearing, the scandal that led up to it, and the line of questions regarding what kind of company Facebook is in reality – is important for anyone who wants to understand the contemporary media landscape and the information ecosystems that make up the public spheres not only in the US, but almost everywhere. Consequently, Walden's questions and Zuckerberg's answer are important when trying to understand the nature of *digital journalism studies*. This field of research – digital journalism studies – has become an important area of study within communications during the last decade because it addresses core questions related to the economy, technology, sociology, culture, language, psychology, and philosophy of what journalism is. It comes at a time when older demarcations – like those between different institutions and companies, between audiences and professionals, practices and perceptions, production and consumption, technologies and humans, physical and virtual, private and public, facts and fictions, truth and lies, and many more – no longer seem valid.

The significance of Facebook and other global platforms and tech companies unknown to the world before the turn of the millennium cannot be overestimated. They constitute a major reason why digital journalism studies is heavily influenced by what Ahva and Steensen (2017) label a "discourse of deconstruction", in which it has become essential to ask fundamental questions concerning what journalism is. Let us offer a few examples of how this discourse of deconstruction has been articulated during the formative years of digital journalism studies as a research field. Anderson (2013) argued that the classical newsroom is no longer the epicenter of newswork and that bloggers, citizen journalists, and social networks are", alongside journalists, important actors in the new "news ecosystem". Peters and Broersma (2013) argued that the problems facing journalism are far more structural than previously suggested, requiring a fundamental rethink about what journalism is. Carlson and Lewis (2015) argued that journalism's demarcations towards other professions and businesses are deconstructed, as are previously established internal boundaries between for instance different journalistic genres, and groups of journalists. And Boczkowski (2011, p. 162) argued for a need to shift "the stance of theoretical work from tributary to primary" in studies focusing on journalism in digital times.

In this book we interrogate the nature of digital journalism studies. We probe the roots from which the field has grown, the technologies, platforms, devices, and audience relations that constitute central objects of study, the theories from which research embarks, the (sometimes) innovative research methods being developed, and the normative underpinnings and possible futures of the field. It is our early contention that digital journalism studies is much more than simply the study of journalism produced, distributed, and/or consumed with the aid of digital technologies. Digital journalism is not defined by its relation to technology alone; such a definition "short-circuits a comprehensive picture of journalism", as Zelizer argues (2019, p. 343). The scholarly field of digital journalism studies is built on questions that disrupt everything previously taken for granted concerning media, journalism, and public spheres: What is a media company? Who is responsible for what is published in a public sphere? What is the difference between those who produce, those who distribute, and those who consume media content, including journalism? And indeed who is a journalist and what is journalism in this complex media and information ecosystem of the 21st century? In search for answers to such questions, digital journalism studies also moves beyond journalism studies and constitutes a cross-disciplinary field that does not focus on journalism only from the traditions of journalism studies, but is open to research from, and conversations with, related fields.

In this introduction, we first look at four structural premises for why questions such as those posed in the previous paragraph are relevant today, and why they matter for digital journalism studies. These structural premises are related to the economy, audience relations, and the networked distribution and consumption mechanisms of digital journalism. We then argue that a fundamental development for digital journalism studies is the way in which news has become separated from journalism since the 1990s. The chapter outlines some empirical characteristics of what digital journalism studies looks like today, as it is presented in the most important arena through which the field materialises, namely the journal *Digital Journalism*. Finally, we present the outline of the book.

1.1 Four structural premises for digital journalism studies

The 2018 Facebook hearing offers an interesting way to begin exploring the topics introduced briefly above not only because it was such an exceptional example of how older and familiar categories of – and demarcations between – different types of companies seem no longer valid, but also because of the scandal leading up to it, the Cambridge Analytica scandal. This revealed the disruptive changes around how information flows in our digital age – changes that have severe consequences for journalism.

The scandal revealed that Facebook had provided access to personal data from 87 million Facebook users to the Cambridge Analytica political consulting and data analytics firm. It also highlighted the enormous potential for how user data can be exploited for both commercial and political gains without users' knowledge or consent along with the ensuing privacy protection issues (Isaak & Hanna, 2018). The scandal was a demonstration of the consequences of what Manovich (2018) has labelled the media analytics stage of modern technological media. It has become evident that the real value of global platform companies like Google, Amazon, and Facebook, as well as Asian platforms such as WeChat and Weibo, lies in their sophisticated methods for harvesting, analysing, and capitalising from tremendous amounts of big data on user behaviour. These methods empower the platform companies with knowledge and insights advertisers are willing to pay for, but also with a wider control over cultural and social networks (Taplin, 2017). The implications of this for journalism have been:

1   A massive shift and crisis in revenue models because advertisers have migrated to platform companies (see for instance Kaye & Quinn, 2010), while news publishers nowadays typically get most of their revenue from their readers.
2   An increased emphasis on user data and audience analytics and metrics in journalism (Belair-Gagnon & Holton, 2018; Cherubini & Nielsen, 2016; Ferrer-Conill & Tandoc, 2018).
3   Shifting patterns of distribution in which companies non-proprietary to institutions of journalism have gained dominance (see for instance Kalsnes & Larsson, 2018; WAN-IFRA, 2019; Westlund & Ekström, 2018).

These three implications are important structural premises for digital journalism studies as an academic field. Moreover, the Cambridge Analytica scandal highlighted another aspect that has dominated much of recent debates in public, industry, and academic discourses on journalism and news; namely problems related to disinformation, "fake news", and trust in the media. Cambridge Analytica used the Facebook data and other data to target US citizens with bespoke political propaganda during the 2016 presidential election campaign and in other elections around the world, including the UK Brexit vote. Reports following the scandal revealed that the company had included disinformation and other forms of information manipulation in their propaganda campaigns, and a tsunami of revelations of similar disinformation campaigns followed (Posetti & Matthews, 2018). This has become a severe problem for journalism, not only because fake news is difficult to disentangle from real news, but also because in another dimension of fake news discourse, the term is used to discredit what is often legitimate news (Egelhofer & Lecheler, 2019). This dimension is seen in President Trump's "fake news"/"fake media" rhetoric towards legacy news institutions – a rhetoric adopted by other state leaders and politicians around the world (such as in Brazil and Nicaragua), in addition to activists and interest groups, most notably those belonging to the political far right. In sum, the two dimensions of fake news hurt journalism because "the media's dependence on social media, analytics and metrics, sensationalism, novelty over newsworthiness, and clickbait makes them vulnerable to such media manipulation" (Marwick & Lewis, 2017, p. 1). In other words: the three implications for journalism based on the structural developments in the digital media and information landscape highlighted above – the disruptive changes in the media economy; the emphasis on audience analytics and metrics; and changing distribution patterns – create a fourth implication:

4   Journalism has become more vulnerable to manipulation, disinformation, and a consequent lack of public trust.

One response by news publishers has been an increased emphasis on institutionalising practices of fact checking and information verification (Graves, 2018), which in turn has created increased interest in both industry and the academy in questions of epistemology: how journalists produce knowledge claims, how they deal with uncertainty, what counts as truthful information, and how all this is affected by the developments in digital media and information technology (Amazeen, 2015; Ekström & Westlund, 2019a; Eldridge II & Bødker, 2019; Steensen, 2019). Moreover, increased distrust in legacy news institutions has given rise to new branches of alternative media and news outlets, especially from the political far right, with different epistemologies (Figenschou & Ihlebæk, 2019; Holt, Ustad Figenschou, & Frischlich, 2019; Nygaard, 2019). The so-called five W's (who, what, where, when, and why) have recurrently been applied for thoughtful analyses about digital journalism studies (Tandoc, 2019b; Waisbord, 2019), and there have been ongoing efforts into the study and debate of key issues such as: what is news, who is a journalist, who are peripheral actors, and what is their role and power in practice (Ahva, 2019; Chua & Duffy, 2019; Eldridge, 2019). Such studies and debates are not merely academic exercises but can have a fundamental impact on who gets to produce and distribute news, and whether media policy enforces functions for support or disabling. More specifically, authorities can take charge over definitions concerning who is a journalist, and who produces misinformation (Belair-Gagnon, Holton, & Westlund, 2019), while platform companies have avoided defining themselves as publishers and thereby are not responsible for editorial content published and distributed on their platforms (Gillespie, 2018).

These four premises, together with the confusion concerning which companies play which roles related to the production, distribution, consumption, and technological facilitation of news, form the structural backbone of digital journalism studies. They inform investigations into the whos, whats, whens, and wheres of contemporary journalism and they call into question previously established knowledge on what journalism is, who counts as a journalist, and what role journalism plays in societies and for the people.

1.2 The separation of news from journalism

The four premises discussed above would not have materialised without one key change in modern media landscapes and public spheres: the ways in which news has become increasingly separated from journalism. When the two authors of this book grew up in Norway (Steensen) and Sweden (Westlund) during the 1970 and 80s, news was inseparably tied to journalism. News was delivered in national newspapers that landed on our doorsteps every morning, in local newspapers delivered by paper boys and girls every afternoon, and, most importantly, through the evening news broadcast by the national public broadcasters NRK (Norway) and SVT and SR (Sweden). Accessing the news was routine. It was delivered in fixed and recognisable formats at specific times and places and it was produced, distributed, and consumed in ritual manners (Carey, 1992).

Journalism is still very much bound by ritual, especially in how it covers events in the world and constructs and upholds social norms and cultural values in a given society (Peters, 2019b). But news is no longer tied to journalism in the same way. News has become dislocated from the proprietary platforms of news companies (Ekström & Westlund, 2019b) and news rituals have expanded way beyond the production, distribution, and consumption of journalism. This separation of news from journalism began with the popularisation of the World Wide Web during the 1990s and what Manovich (2018) calls "the Web as global content creation and distribution network" stage in the development of modern technological media. With the web, journalistic institutions lost their almost monopolistic position as providers of news to mass audiences, since everyone could now set up a web page, create content, and distribute it to a public audience. Governments, public bodies, political parties, politicians, private enterprises, NGOs, and other kinds of institutions could set up their own news services through the web and bypass journalists; so could private individuals. Some individuals were very successful, like the former telemarketer Matt Drudge who in 1996 started publishing the *Drudge Report*, which became a highly influential news provider and political commentary website in the US (Leetaru, 2009).

The separation of news from journalism escalated when the blog format became popular in the early 2000s. Blogs allowed individuals with limited tech savviness to set up news services with little effort and cost, and marked the beginning of the social media platforms stage of modern technological media (Manovich, 2018), in which discourses of participation (Singer et al., 2011), user-generated content creation and utilisation (Ornebring, 2008; Thurman, 2008), and citizen reporting (Allan & Thorsen, 2009) became popular in both journalism and journalism studies. This created a situation in which the boundaries between those who produce and those who consume news became blurred and coalesced in "produsage" (Bruns, 2010). Combined with the massive industrial changes in the media landscape and economy globally (exemplified with the rise of Facebook and Google), technological innovation, distribution, and social interaction became the new kings (Albarran, 2016) who provided a forceful push towards separating news from journalism.

Today, news is something that you find in formats and on platforms of your own choosing. News is more often than not deprived of edited contexts and fixed genres and formats, and reaches you in mash-ups containing journalistic news, public relations news, advertisements, news from politicians, celebrities, sports idols, and artists, personal news from your friends and family, professional news from your colleagues and professional associations, and perhaps also fake news from bots. These news mash-ups, which typically reach you in social media feeds, are personalised interfaces with an abundance of information floating around in bits and pieces in a gigantic, digital network. Journalism is one among these sources that both build on each other and are increasingly difficult to separate from one another for the end-user. News used to be fixed in time, space, culture, materiality, and patterns of production, distribution, and consumption. Now news is networked (C. W. Anderson, 2013; Domingo, Masip, & Costera Meijer, 2015; A. Russell, 2013). It exists in information "ecosystems" (Picard, 2014) with strong or weak connections to journalism, connections that might be difficult to detect.

1.3 What does *Digital Journalism* studies look like?

Throughout the book we will assess the development of the field through a systematic review of articles published in journals, most notably the journal which has most shaped the field, *Digital Journalism*. This journal was launched in 2013 to be a "critical forum for the scholarly discussion, analysis and responses to the wide-ranging implications of digital technologies for the practice and study of journalism" (Franklin, 2013, p. 1). *Digital Journalism* quickly became a highly influential journal, not only within journalism studies, but also within the broader discipline of communication. Table 1.1 displays citation metrics and rankings within the discipline of communication of the five most influential journalism journals internationally: *Digital Journalism*, *Journalism – Theory, Practice & Criticism*, *Journalism Studies*, *Journalism Practice*, and *Journalism & Mass Communication Quarterly*. Even though *Digital Journalism* is the youngest of these journals, it became the highest-ranked journalism journal by quite a large margin in 2018. This journal is therefore important to assess when analysing the nature of digital journalism studies and its development.

Steensen and colleagues (2019) have previously conducted a content analysis of *Digital Journalism* in order to assess what digital journalism studies, as portrayed in this journal, looks like, and also of other journalism journals

Table 1.1 2018 citation metrics and ranking within the discipline of communication from SJR (SCImago Journal Ranking), Scopus, and Google Scholar. The table displays the five top journalism journals.

Journal	SJR		Google citations		Scopus	
	Rank	Impact factor	Rank	H5 Index	Rank	CiteScore
Digital Journalism	9	2,67	5	44	5	4,55
Journalism TP&C	19	1,62	9	39	19	2,98
Journalism Studies	20	1,55	10	38	26	2,74
Journalism Practice	27	1,36	11	36	32	2,53
Journalism & Mass Comm. Q	29	1,32	17	32	25	2,74

to determine degrees of interdisciplinarity and theoretical perspectives used in journalism studies in general (Ahva & Steensen, 2020; Steensen & Ahva, 2015). We build further on these analyses and present findings throughout this book, predominantly based on the analysis of keywords used to tag the articles published in *Digital Journalism* from the first issue in 2013 to issue 4, 2019, abstracts of the same articles, the references cited in them, and the nationality of the articles' authors. For those who are interested in the methodological procedures behind the analysis, we have added an online appendix where these procedures are laid out and discussed.

We will briefly discuss two aspects of this analysis in this introductory chapter: the interdisciplinarity of digital journalism studies, and the degrees to which the field is globally diverse.

1.3.1 The interdisciplinarity of digital journalism studies

In an introductory essay to a special issue discussing definitions of both digital journalism and its study, the editorial team of *Digital Journalism* argue that viewing digital journalism studies as a sub-field of journalism studies "limits its value and potential to scholarship not just within media studies and communication, but its wider interdisciplinary reach" (Eldridge II, Hess, Tandoc, & Westlund, 2019, p. 393). The interdisciplinarity of digital journalism studies is in other words a key characteristic of the field, according to the editorial team. However, journalism studies is also reckoned to be an interdisciplinary field and the question therefore becomes to what degree the two fields differ in their interdisciplinarity.

Journalism studies is a young academic field rooted in the social sciences and the humanities. It is traditionally marked by approaches and perspectives from sociology, political science, cultural studies, language studies, and history (Zelizer, 2004). In a longitudinal analysis of disciplinary perspectives found in abstracts of articles published in the journals *Journalism Studies* and *Journalism – Theory, Practice & Criticism* from 2000 to 2013, Steensen and Ahva (2015) found that sociology was the main source of influence in journalism studies and that this discipline had become increasingly dominant. Political science perspectives, which dominated the field in the early 2000s, was the second most common discipline, while cultural studies, language studies, and history played minor parts. In addition, fields and disciplines like business and administration, economics, law, and philosophy were present, while technological perspectives were on the rise.

The question then is whether *digital* journalism studies is marked by the same disciplinary patterns as journalism studies, or if it has different sources of influence. The discussion in section 1.1 of the premises that form the backbone of the field suggests that digital journalism studies draws on a wider range of perspectives than journalism studies, given digital journalism's influences from and orientation towards practices, professions, institutions, technologies, and cultures beyond journalism, and given the field's emphasis on *change* as a formative concept (Peters & Carlson, 2019), a point we will discuss more thoroughly in chapter 6, section 6.2.2. However, recent reviews reveal that there is a discrepancy between this expected level of interdisciplinarity in digital journalism studies and the actual research being conducted within the field. Boczkowski and Mitchelstein (2017) argue that digital journalism studies is marked by two limitations: 1) the ability to connect empirical findings from digital journalism studies across other domains of digital culture, and 2) a lack of conceptual exchanges with other fields and disciplines. Steensen and colleagues (2019) found similar tendencies and argued that digital journalism studies could benefit from more inclusion of perspectives from the humanities, and of theoretical and not only methodological perspectives from information science and computer science.

Figure 1.1 displays the disciplinary perspectives that dominate abstracts of articles published in *Digital Journalism* (see online appendix for details on methodology). One third of the abstracts analysed draw primarily on sociological frameworks, making this the most common disciplinary

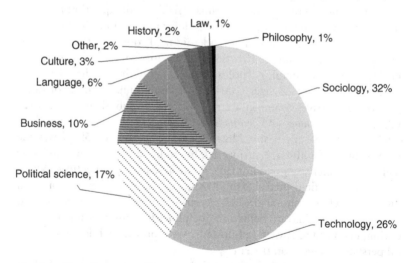

Perspectives in *Digital Journalism* abstracts 2013-2019

Figure 1.1 Share of the most dominant disciplinary perspectives in abstracts of articles published in *Digital Journalism* from issue 1, volume 1 (2013) to issue 4, volume 7 (2019). Every second abstract is analysed (N = 172). See online appendix for details on methodology.

perspective. This is quite similar to the dominance of sociology in journalism studies in general, as is the share of articles based primarily on a political science framework (Ahva & Steensen, 2020; Steensen & Ahva, 2015). The difference between articles published in *Digital Journalism* and in other journalism journals is that technological perspectives are much more common in *Digital Journalism*, where they dominate every fourth article. Another difference is that disciplines from the humanities, such as cultural studies, language studies, history studies, and philosophy, are less common in articles published in *Digital Journalism* than in other journalism journals.

We will return to these interdisciplinary characteristics of digital journalism studies and what they mean in several chapters throughout this book, especially in chapters 5 and 7. For now we will conclude that there are both similarities and differences in the ways in which digital journalism studies and journalism studies are interdisciplinary.

1.3.2 Digital journalism studies and global diversity

The Facebook hearings in 2018 illustrate a key dimension of the modern media and technology landscape: it is inherently global. Facebook and other platform companies within the media and technology industries know few national boundaries, with notable exceptions like China, in which Facebook and Google are banned. Nonetheless, the big platform companies have global outreach, as do the infrastructure that facilitates their existence, the internet and the World Wide Web. The Cambridge Analytica scandal was also of global proportions, since this company had not only interfered in the 2016 presidential elections in the US, but allegedly in more than 200 elections worldwide, including in Argentina, Nigeria, Kenya, India, and the Czech Republic (Posetti & Matthews, 2018, p. 14).

Digital journalism, which is facilitated by the same globalised infrastructure everywhere, is almost by default a global phenomenon. Bob Franklin, the founding editor of *Digital Journalism*, proclaimed that a core commitment of the journal's editorial policy would be to appreciate a multitude of geographical contexts, which would imply seeking out

> studies which explore developments in digital journalism in those regions of the globe which typically do not enjoy the same access to the debating chamber constituted by western-based journals that is enjoyed by scholars and journalists in the developed global north.
>
> (Franklin, 2013, p. 3)

Digital Journalism has in recent years taken steps towards global diversities in terms of who has been invited to join the quite large and diverse editorial board, where the journal encourages submissions from, and where it would like to engage both academics and other audiences. Concerning the latter point, the 2019 appointment of three international engagement editors in the US, Chile, and Singapore is a clear sign of the journal's ambition towards global outreach and diversity. However, the journal has not (yet) managed to live up to this commitment in terms of where authors come from, at least not compared to the other journalism journals, which have a more globally diverse set of authors. Figure 1.2 displays an overview of the parts of the world first authors of articles published in the five top-ranked journalism journals represent. Ninety percent of the *Digital Journalism* first authors are based in North America or Western Europe, making it the most Western-centric of the five journals.

Diversity is a topic we will explore in several chapters in this book: in chapter 2, where we introduce an analytical framework for understanding the relationship between digital journalism and its object of inquiry (see section 2.2); in chapters 3 and 4, where we unpack the diversity of the objects of study in digital journalism studies; and in chapters 5 and 6, where we discuss theoretical and methodological diversity. These discussions will undoubtedly reveal that digital journalism studies is a very diverse field and that its premises and founding principles assume a global perspective and research agenda. That said, by way of published articles in these five journals, the field remains dominated by scholars based in North America and Western Europe. In this context it is worth remembering that there are numerous additional journals producing large amounts of research associated with specific geographical regions, such as *African Journalism Studies*, *Asian Journal of Communication*, *Brazilian Journalism Research*, and *Chinese Journal of Communication*, to mention some key examples of journals from the beginning of the alphabet.

1.4   Outline of the book

This book comprises eight chapters, which in their survey of the historical origins of digital journalism studies to its possible futures, explore in more detail the topics raised briefly in this introduction. In chapter 2, "The Definitions: Current Debates and a Framework for Assessing Digital Journalism Studies", we argue that the origins of digital journalism studies lie in the research that has explored the historic relationship between journalism and technology. The chapter revisits this relationship, before moving towards the current debates on how to define both digital journalism and digital journalism studies. The chapter also introduces a framework to analyse the relationship between the academic field and its object of inquiry, a framework consisting of three dimensions: society, sector, and scholarship.

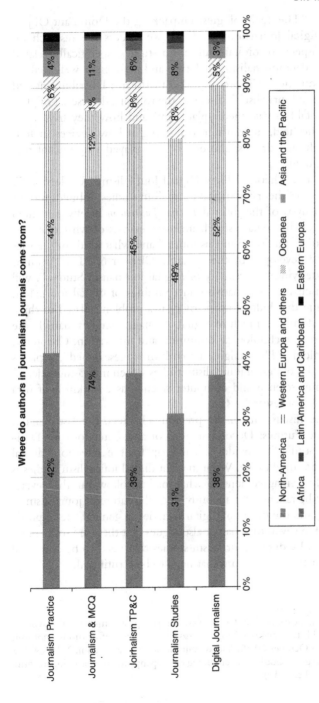

Figure 1.2 First authors of all articles published in the journals *Digital Journalism, Journalism, Journalism Studies, Journalism: TP&C, Journalism & Mass Communication Quarterly,* and *Journalism Practice* during the years 2013–2019. Definitions of the regions are based on the UN Regional groups.

Note: Data from 2013 and 2014 for *Journalism Practice* was not available. N = 1989 (no. of articles). See online appendix for details on methodology.

In chapter 3, "The Technologies: Unpacking the Dominant Object of Study in Digital Journalism Studies", we discuss the research on technological aspects of digital journalism studies, specifically related to the topics of data journalism, analytics, and metrics, as well as algorithms and automation. Chapter 4, "The Platforms: Distributions and Devices in Digital Journalism", discusses the role of a diverse set of platforms (most notably social media platforms) and how they have been researched in the field, in addition to looking at how devices such as tablets, smart phones, drones, and others have played a significant role in the research field.

Chapter 5, "The Theories: How Digital Journalism is Understood", considers the role of theory in digital journalism studies. It builds further on the meta-analysis of the journal *Digital Journalism* briefly presented in this chapter, as this meta-research includes analysis of what role theory plays in articles published in this journal and what kinds of theories are adopted and developed by the research. Chapter 6, "The Assumptions: The Underlying Normativity of Digital Journalism Studies", will unmask and discuss the normative underpinnings of digital journalism studies and argue that hidden normativity is a problem related to three discourses that dominate much of digital journalism studies, namely the discourses of crisis, technological optimism, and innovation. Chapter 7, "The Methodologies: How Digital Journalism is Researched", explores the methodologies of digital journalism studies which increasingly derive from information science and computer science as new kinds of data become available for researchers.

Based on the discussions in the previous chapters, the last chapter, chapter 8, "The Futures: Deconstructions of and Directions for Digital Journalism Studies", provides a road map for the directions digital journalism studies might take. We argue that digital journalism studies is not best served by an agreement on what road to follow, but that several directions must be taken simultaneously since the future of journalism in our digital age, and the future of digital societies in general, are impossible to predict. However, the chapter also argues that there are some blind spots left behind by digital journalism studies that need to be addressed and some normative assumptions that need to be scrutinised.

Note

1 Transcript of the hearings found at www.washingtonpost.com/news/the-switch/wp/2018/04/11/transcript-of-zuckerbergs-appearance-before-house-committee/ (accessed 3 October 2019). Video available at www.cnbc.com/2018/04/11/mark-zuckerberg-facebook-is-a-technology-company-not-media-company.html (accessed 3 October 2019).

2 The definitions

Current debates and a framework for assessing digital journalism studies

In recent years a great number of journalism studies scholars have developed research agendas which are increasingly oriented towards digital journalism. They have been joined by scholars from many different fields including, but not limited to, computer science, political communication, media management, mobile media, and communication. This chapter discusses the parallel emergence of digital journalism studies as a field, and digital journalism as a practice. Here we discuss the roots and current developments of digital journalism studies, as well as important debates, approaches, and definitions of the field. The chapter presents an analytical framework that, going forward, allows us to further our understanding of how research about digital journalism corresponds with developments in digital journalism. Core questions for this chapter are: Where does digital journalism studies come from? How can it be defined? And how does it interplay with changes in society and the journalism sector?

2.1 Digital journalism studies: definitions and debates

Both digital journalism and digital journalism studies are contested and widely discussed concepts, which also represent "moving targets" that change over time. Scholars disagree about what digital journalism and digital journalism studies "are", and it is a daunting task to do justice to the different and diverse positions and nuances. We will nevertheless attempt to outline some key aspects and arguments. Digital journalism studies has been influenced by many fields but has largely emerged from journalism studies, which in turn can be placed within the larger discipline of communication (Carlson, Robinson, Lewis, & Berkowitz, 2018). Importantly, though, scholars have proposed to approach digital journalism studies as a field of its own, drawing not only on its well-established links to disciplines such as communication, political communication, sociology, and economics, but also on fields more focused on "digital" aspects, such as computer science and information science (cf. Eldridge II et al., 2019). We stress that this obviously means that scholars can apply and develop other approaches to their epistemological processes of producing scientific knowledge. By approaching digital journalism studies as a field of its own, it can evolve more openly without abiding to the ways-of-doing largely established within journalism studies, and which may create certain expectations and path-dependencies.

The most recent and systematic effort towards advancing this discussion is to be found in a special issue in *Digital Journalism* published in 2019 titled "Defining Digital Journalism (Studies)". The *Digital Journalism* editorial team invited a number of scholars from different parts of the world who could offer different viewpoints, arguments, and discussion around the shape of the field. Table 2.1 presents us with the concise definitions offered by each of these contributors. The special issue starts with a definition of digital journalism based on an empirical review and analysis of the field, continues with five conceptual articles, and ends with a synthesis by the members of the editorial team, discussing nuances in the different approaches and definitions (Eldridge II et al., 2019). One key aspect concerns the role of digital technologies in relation to journalism. As Zelizer (2019) highlights, journalism is a cultural practice and scholars should not overemphasise the role played by digital technology. Other contributors offer arguments about how to think of digital technology in ways that go beyond seeing them as tools and systems, but rather as embedded in a broader set of socio-technical dynamics. Contributing scholars highlight that the digital is transcendental (Robinson, Lewis, & Carlson, 2019), transforming and/or expanding journalism (Steensen et al., 2019; Waisbord, 2019), and playing an important role in bringing forward new rules and processes (Duffy & Ang, 2019).

Both authors of this book have also been involved in forwarding definitions to this debate. The first author (Steensen) was lead author on a review article for the above-mentioned special issue of *Digital Journalism*, offering a -multidimensional assessment of all articles published in the journal from 2013 until mid-2018, and thus providing an empirically based definition that stresses mutual dependence with digital technology and a symbiotic relationship with audiences (Steensen et al., 2019). The article calls for greater awareness of the different kinds of knowledge that digital journalism studies scholars produce. This chapter attempts to address that void. Moreover, the second author (Westlund) coauthored the definition forwarded by the *Digital Journalism* editorial team, proposing their normative approach to digital journalism studies for the journal. They introduced the "The Digital Journalism Studies Compass" (the DJS

Table 2.1 Definitions of digital journalism and digital journalism studies discussed in a special issue of *Digital Journalism*. The table was originally published in Eldridge II et al. (2019, p. 392).

Steen Steensen, Anna M. Grøndahl Larsen, Ynqve Benestad Hågvar and Birgitte Kjos Fonn, 2019, 338
Digital journalism is the transforming social practice of selecting, interpreting, editing and distributing factual information of perceived public interest to various kinds of audiences in specific, but changing genres and formats. As such, digital journalism both shapes and is shaped by new technologies and platforms, and it is marked by an increasingly symbiotic relationship with the audiences. The actors engaged in this social practice are bound by the structures of social institutions publicly recognized as journalistic Institutions

Sue Robinson, Seth C. Lewis and Matt Carlson, 2019, 369-370	Andrew Duffy and Ang Peng Hwa, 2019, 382	Silvio Waisbord, 2019, 352	Jean Burgess and Edward Hurcombe, 2019, 360	Barbie Zelizer, 2019, 349
Research that involves newswork employing digital technologies in some manner, such as news websites, social platforms, mobile devices, data analytics, algorithms, etc.; Research that acknowledges how digital dynamics of journalism interact with and alter formerly discrete boundaries . . . and the authority and forces that go along	Digital journalism as the way in which journalism embodies the philosophies, norms, practices, values and attitudes of digitisation as they relate to society. These include the efficiency of control, storage, retrieval, accessibility and transmission of data; indusivity, interactivity and collaboration in the propagation of information and	Digital journalism is the networked production, distribution and consumption of news and information. It is characterized by network settings and practices that expand the opportunities and spaces for news	Those practices of newsgathering, reporting, textual production and ancillary communication that reflect, respond to, and shape the social, cultural and economic logics of the constantly changing digital media environment. To study digital journalism is to study the transformative and isomorphic impacts of digital media technologies and business models on the practice, product and business of journalism, as well as the ways that	Digital journalism thus takes its meaning from both practice and rhetoric. Its practice as newsmaking embodies a set of expectations, practices, capabilities and limitations relative to those associated with pre-digital and non-digital forms, reflecting a difference of degree rather than kind. Its rhetoric heralds the hopes and anxieties associated with sustaining the journalistic enterprise as worthwhile. With the

(*Continued*)

Table 2.1 (Continued)

with these changes and configurations; Research that interrogates the resulting practical and cultural transformations occurring around news and other acts of journalism as they relate to broader issues . . .	opinion; flexibility and innovation in presenting news stories; and state, institutional and individual ownership of data and its implications for privacy and transparency	journalistic discourses, practices and logics in turn shape the cultures and technologies of those digital media platforms through which journalism is practiced, and its products are shared and consumed	digital comprising the figure to journalism's ground, digital journalism constitutes the most recent of many conduits over time that have allowed us to imagine optimum links between journalism and its publics

Scott Eldridge, Kristy Hess, Edson Tandoc, and Oscar Westlund, 2019, 394.

Digital Journalism Studies should strive to be an academic field which critically explores, documents, and explains the interplay of digitization and journalism, continuity and change.

Digital Journalism Studies should further strive to focus, conceptualize, and theorize tensions, configurations, power imbalances, and the debates these continue to raise for digital journalism and its futures.

Compass) as a visual and metaphorical tool that can help guide scholars in navigating the interrelationships between "digital" and "journalism" on the one end, and "continuity" and "change" on the other. Their emphasis on "continuity" seeks to make sure scholarship builds on existing knowledge, theories, and concepts, while "change" opens for cutting-edge scholarship that pushes these boundaries (Eldridge II et al., 2019).

2.2 An analytical framework: society, sector, and scholarship

This discussion of debates in the field extends into the nature of the relationship between researchers and their objects of study. Therefore, we have developed an analytical framework that helps visualise and explain developments in digital journalism vis-à-vis digital journalism studies. This framework encompasses three core dimensions: A) *society*, B) *sector*, and C) *scholarship*.

With *society* we refer to how the world changes at a global, national, and local level, including but not limited to political, economic, social, and technological factors. While this dimension is very important, this book does not aspire to discuss such changes in close detail. Our purpose with introducing the society dimension into the analytical framework has to do with its relevance for discussions of the two other dimensions. The second dimension, *sector*, encompasses journalism as a phenomenon and institution, as a market and industry, as well as a profession, practice, service, and product. The *society* (A) and *sector* (B) dimensions represent what theory of science would refer to as ontology. This concept refers to reality and existence, essentially what the world *is*, and what can be said to exist. From our perspective, the journalism sector clearly exists and continuously changes in relation to society. The conditions surrounding the "reality" of the journalism sector have been measured, studied, discussed, and approached in multiple ways. There are of course "facts" in the world, such as when news publisher company X makes redundant Y number of journalists on a specific date. We tend to see such occurrences as facts based on widely agreed upon principles for the calendar system and mathematics. However, things become less straightforward when we turn to questions of the antecedents to why these journalists were sacked. Was it because of poor leadership? Or because of publishers' loss of revenue to platform companies? Or was it perhaps a mix of these factors, and many more? Members of the journalism sector attempt to resolve such questions as they navigate these challenges, and so do researchers in fields such as digital journalism studies. Importantly, we subscribe to the position that scholars socially construct accounts of reality, whereby assessing these factors we are better able to gain a picture of the "reality" associated with journalism. Thus, we engage in epistemological processes of producing scientific knowledge about complex and continuously evolving changes in society and the journalism sector as they intertwine. The *scholarship* (C) dimension thus has to do with the epistemologies with which scholars produce knowledge.

This analytical framework helps to illuminate the interrelationship between the journalism *sector* and *scholarship* on digital journalism studies and can guide analyses and discussion of whether the journalism sector and digital journalism studies scholars have focused on similar or dissimilar questions. The components of the analytical framework are brought into discussions of research in thematic clusters in chapter 3 and 4, and has inspired our conclusions and directions in chapter 8.

We ask you to imagine a timeline with different milestones that have had major, perhaps even disruptive, effects on journalism. For example, imagine for a moment how (A) developments in the telecom sector have influenced society and (B) the journalism sector, as well as specific news publishers, and (C) subsequently also generated numerous studies in digital journalism studies. Diffusion of mobile telephony substantially improved journalistic fieldwork and the possibilities for getting in touch with sources. The launch of the Apple mobile ecosystem with native apps in 2007, and thereafter the Android mobile operating systems, spurred substantial shifts when it comes to how the journalism sector publishes news, and how citizens access the news (Westlund, 2013). Mobile communication is a taken-for-granted part of society (Ling, 2012), and mobile devices offer ubiquitous access to citizens, presenting publishers with both opportunities and challenges. Indeed, cross-cultural surveys show that most people use smartphones as their main gateway for news and that people use social media platforms more generally to access news (Newman, Fletcher, Kalogeropoulos, & Nielsen, 2019). Notwithstanding this, research into mobile journalism and mobile news remains relatively limited. Studies into newsrooms and newswork have typically focused on "online" in general, largely overlooking approaches and practices related to "mobile" devices and aspects (see review in Westlund & Quinn, 2018). This area of research, discussed further in chapter 4, remains relatively fertile ground although news publishers have experimented with mobile news more or less as long as they have with social media.

To return to our framework of *society* (A), *sector* (B), and *scholarship* (C), we wish to highlight that although mobile media and communication have gained significance in society and the journalism sector (A+B), relatively few publications have focused on, or even considered, such aspects and developments. Ultimately, we argue that A+B disconnects with C when it comes to how stakeholders in each camp have focused their attention. This discussion of mobile technologies and communication, as but one example of research in the field, shows how such disconnections influence the knowledge production in, and thereby epistemologies of, digital journalism studies.

Our contribution in this chapter, however, does *not* sit within an effort towards offering an empirical, systematic, and comprehensive analysis of the interplay between society, sector, and scholarship. Instead, we turn now towards unpacking the interrelationship between these three dimensions by introducing four key mechanisms: 1) Issue (in)visibility, 2) Pro-innovation bias, 3) Path dependency, and 4) Addressability. The first focuses on issue (in)visibility in the journalism sector (B), whereas the second (pro-innovation bias) and third (path dependency) apply to both the journalism sector (B) and to digital journalism studies (C). The fourth mechanism, addressability, mainly applies to digital journalism studies. We will now introduce each of these four dimensions and continue by building on our example of mobile news.

2.2.1 *Issue (in)visibility*

The nature of visibility and invisibility concerning what happens in the journalism sector (B) varies substantially. Representatives from the journalism sector may deliberately draw a lot of attention to certain innovations by the news industry. For example, industry members have taken pride in building their social media presence, increasing audience engagement, and developing and launching mobile applications. They have communicated about such developments quite broadly and publicly, including in industry press and trade magazines, public talks, and in the news itself where they pitch such developments towards their audiences. By contrast, other issues have been largely invisible, like how the journalism sector addresses challenges relating to digital safety, including safe communication with sources, online harassment, hacks, and surveillance. Exceptions include handbook chapters covering such issues (Franklin & Eldridge II, 2017), and *Digital Journalism* has also published a special issue focusing on surveillance (Wahl-Jorgensen, Hintz, Dencik, & Bennett, 2017).

Moreover, we posit that issue (in)visibility in the journalism sector (B) influences the extent to which different stakeholders learn from and mimic each other (labelled: isomorphism and herd behaviour), as well as the extent to which digital journalism scholars (C) conduct research into specific areas. The mechanism is relational: high visibility in the sector (B+) likely results in more digital journalism scholarship (C+), whereas invisibility (B-) reduces the chances of such issues being researched (C-).

Turning back to the example of mobile news we argue that while mobile applications were central objects of inquiry during the formative years of smartphones and tablets with touchscreen, they have since been appropriated and normalised. Invisibility for journalists, as a consequence, increases when their news organisations incorporate mobile into their cross-media approaches, using content management systems (CMS) that are designed to effortlessly publish across desktop, tablet, and smartphone sites and apps (e.g., Erdal, Vaage Øie, Oppegaard, & Westlund, 2019; Westlund, 2014). As a result, publishing across platforms can be something journalists do not need to think about in their daily practice, nor something they have wide awareness of or talk about. In extension of this, practice-oriented researchers studying routines among journalists in newsrooms may well not see concrete practices associated with mobile devices taking place (Westlund & Ekström, 2020), and thus not highlighted in studies of appropriation and normalisation of technologies into newsrooms (Coddington, 2014; Djerf-Pierre, Ghersetti, & Hedman, 2016). We should add that many industry associations have devoted panels to mobile in their conferences and workshops, and in their media innovation work, albeit its role and significance does not necessarily surface in everyday newswork. Ultimately, mobile news in the journalism sector may have been largely invisible to digital journalism scholars conducting ethnographic research, utilising interviews, mapping affordances, analysing content on websites, and so forth.

2.2.2 Pro-innovation bias

Innovation as a concept refers to both the development and the implementation of something "new", which can be processes, products, services, and other things (Storsul & Krumsvik, 2013b). There is a pro-innovation bias associated with all three aspects of our framework that rests on fundamental drivers of capitalism where, in order to maintain a competitive advantage, companies and nations have incentives to continuously develop their products, services, and so forth. Such drivers are continuously changing society and market sectors. We see this in the ways news publishers began experimenting with and innovating for the World Wide Web a quarter of a century ago, developing different approaches to, and practices for, online journalism. We also see this in the way media managers and journalists in the sector, as well as scholars in digital journalism studies and beyond, have repeatedly discussed that legacy news media in the Western world (especially those formerly known as newspapers) essentially "need to" innovate (Aitamurto & Lewis, 2013; Pavlik, 2013; Storsul & Krumsvik, 2013a). Scholars from diverse fields have focused on "innovation" as a concept and object of inquiry, even as they also found a great deal of heterogeneity and uncertainty surrounding the bounds of this concept (Bleyen, Lindmark, Ranaivoson, & Ballon, 2014).

However, common denominators have emerged, and these involve developing something new, possibly by combining different parts previously held apart (Storsul & Krumsvik, 2013b). While companies in different sectors often strive towards innovation, scholars have shown it may well not be a solution, despite tremendous investments (Seelos & Mair, 2012). Innovation has been problematised by several researchers with a footing in digital journalism studies, arguing (in similar terms) that "innovation, as a general concept, suggests creativeness and success in a competitive environment, and is popularly held as a holy grail, something for which to strive and claim as a source of pride" (Westlund & Lewis, 2014, p. 14). A qualitative study with 39 representatives from news publishers across numerous countries suggests that members of the journalism sector have been overly obsessed with innovation related to "bright, shiny things", and focused less on developing long-term strategies for sustainable innovation (Posetti, 2018).

Scholars have repeatedly advanced rhetorical and normative assumptions around how digital technology may either save or kill the role of journalism and news, and with them, news organisations (see also chapter 6). Essentially the pro-innovation bias mechanism has to do with practitioners in the journalism sector (B) focusing on innovation and emerging technologies that they envision may help them overcome contemporary challenges. In addition, it also sees influential scholars taking the lead in approaching "trending" and "innovative" objects of inquiry such as social media platforms, and many others have followed suit, resulting in tremendous amounts of research publications (see also chapter 4).

2.2.3 Path dependency

What journalists and news organisations do is inexorably linked to their culture and institutionalised routines: essentially the history of how they do things. This results in path dependency. In other words, history constrains the actions taken by having carved out a path, limiting the ways in which journalists and institutions approach emerging opportunities and challenges. Such patterns are found across the journalism sector, with news publishers displaying herd behaviours as they engage in vicarious learning where they follow the moves by peers, including imitating industry leaders. Studies have demonstrated how seemingly predestined approaches to emerging technologies taking shape in one news organisation materialise into something others in the sector take notice of and imitate, and when doing so they are further reinforcing specific paths of development in the journalism sector (Boczkowski, 2010; Westlund, 2012).

Path dependency also surfaces when it comes to how scholars develop and maintain their research agendas. Imagine yourself as a young person embarking in academia to pursue a PhD, getting further training in theories and methods in the discipline. You read and digest massive amounts of research to develop solid research reviews that lead to identifying important research questions, which you study empirically. You develop expertise in that area, and with those methods and theories. If you succeed in academia, you specialise further via various opportunities, including post-docs, tenure-track positions, research projects, and so forth. We dare say few scholars renew themselves substantially, by which we mean develop expertise across multiple theories, multiple methods, and multiple objects of inquiry. Some are making steps towards renewal, whereas some essentially build up their track record by repeatedly applying the same theories and methods for the study of changing patterns (for example by conducting annual surveys or content analyses). These scholars are adding to a reinforcement of scholarly path dependencies influencing the routes embarked by others.

2.2.4 Addressability

The final mechanism, associated with (in)visibility, focuses on what we refer to as addressability. We can address this through the same A (*society*), B (*sector*), C (*scholarship*) framework. Essentially, this has to do with the epistemological challenges that arise when trying to develop research (C) that addresses objects of inquiry in society (A) or the sector (B). While different theories can be used for developing research into a specific object of inquiry, some theories have become more widely used than others by repeatedly being applied to the study of changing conditions in the journalism sector. There is thus a body of literature that demonstrates the addressability of such theories, which other scholars can then build on. However, sometimes well-established theories which were developed in a mass media era are criticised for not harmonising well with conditions and patterns in the contemporary mediascape. There are also theories and traditions found in the humanities, cultural studies, feminist critiques, postcolonial perspectives, and so forth that have relevance, but which few scholars have pushed forward in this context. Nevertheless, digital journalism studies is an interdisciplinary field breaking new terrains, advancing original research into areas that have never been addressed before. In doing so, it may not always be self-evident how to approach these areas theoretically, and while there is a magnitude of theories (see chapter 5), there are also studies published without theoretical frameworks.

Another aspect of addressability has to do with research designs and methods and the epistemic knowledge claims scholars are making based on their empirical studies. In digital journalism studies and beyond there has been much research about "social media" over the past decade, many of which focus on Twitter (partly because the journalism sector has focused relatively much on Twitter as a platform). The Twitter API and the data which can be accessed through it have made Twitter a more accessible platform compared to other social media platforms (though GDPR regulations have resulted in reduced access, particularly in the European Union). As a result, while scholars can take advantage of sound methodologies that allow for the study of Twitter, they must simultaneously remain careful when making knowledge claims and avoid transferring explanations born of analysis of Twitter data onto a wider range of social media use. We conclude that addressability in terms of easily accessible data strongly influences patterns of research publications. We return to this problem in chapter 7 (section 7.2.3).

2.3 Turning to thematic clusters in *Digital Journalism*

Taking as a point of departure the interdisciplinary nature of digital journalism studies, and the empirical analysis of disciplinary perspectives presented in the first chapter (section 1.3.1), the next two chapters will present an analysis of research published in *Digital Journalism* from its inaugural issue in 2013 until issue 4 in 2019. We build further on research previously undertaken by Steensen et al. (2019) and have analysed and sthematised the keywords from a total of 343 original articles published in *Digital Journalism* (see online appendix for details on methodology).

Table 2.2 charts the contours of the digital journalism studies field across a wide range of distinct objects of study, grouping distinct keywords together into so-called thematic clusters. In total there are eleven thematic clusters, representing 65 percent of all keywords used in articles. Three of these thematic clusters are most dominant; *technology* (17 percent), *platform* (13 percent), and *audience* (10 percent). Further, while scholars commonly use theory or method among their keywords, these keywords offer little insight into more specific contributions. Thus, there are only nine thematic clusters building on more specific objects of inquiry, and the remaining six account for only two or three percent each.

Performing assessments of keywords is useful for establishing an overview of patterns in research publications but can quite naturally only take us so far. There are clearly limitations here compared to the more

Table 2.2 Thematic clusters of keywords used in the 343 original articles published in *Digital Journalism* from volume 1, issue 1 (2013) to volume 7, issue 4 (2019) that contained keywords.

Thematic cluster	No. of keywords	Percent of all keywords
Technology	378	17%
Platform	302	13%
Audience	232	10%
Methodology	109	5%
Theory	103	5%
Business	71	3%
Region	73	3%
Genre	63	3%
Philosophy/epistemology	68	3%
Visual	36	2%
Professionalism	43*	2%
Sum	1478	65%
Sum other keywords	779	35%
Sum total	2257	100%

time-demanding assessment of reading and assessing full-length articles. Chapters 3 and 4 will therefore assess and discuss more closely the important patterns and findings from articles associated with the two most dominant thematic clusters; *technology* and *platforms*. Each of these chapters will link the assessments to discussions of research into *audiences*. This is the third most dominant thematic cluster, and is closely interrelated to the two other.

Importantly, we do not claim to offer a systematic review of all literature in the field since digital journalism scholars produce more than 1000 journal articles per year.

3 The technologies

Unpacking the dominant object of study in *Digital Journalism* Studies

Imagine for a moment a legacy news media organisation and how their social actors continuously are trying to make sense of digital technologies, advancing their production and distribution of news. Imagine how this organisation and their journalists, who are used to traditional news reporting techniques, approach the opportunities and challenges at hand when it comes to *data journalism*. What explicit and tacit knowledge do they need, and how should they sorganise data journalism? Should they focus on developing sspecialised teams, or enhancing generalists' knowledge about data journalism? What networks of sources (Ettema & Glasser, 1985) can they rely on in terms of datasets, and what truth claims can they make? How does the organisation approach and make use of audience analytics – the technological systems tracing-patterns of behaviour from digital platforms – and generate metrics from them that can then be acted upon? Will analytics and metrics help the journalists to understand better what news material engages their readers, facilitating conversion into subscriptions? Moreover, can the legacy news organisation's publisher appropriate technologies for automated news distribution and for automated personalisation, and so forth?

These are the sorts of questions that digital journalism studies scholars have addressed throughout the 2010s as part of what we refer to as the technology thematic cluster comprising 378 different keywords associated with the articles published in *Digital Journalism* from issue 1, 2013, to issue 4, 2019. This chapter focuses on a great number of these keywords, joining up this focus with a brief discussion of research associated with the third largest thematic cluster, *Audiences*. The technology thematic cluster encompasses a wide array of keywords that have been dealt with by researchers over the years. We can proceed alphabetically. Starting with A, we find emerging research into the role of *ad-tech* in journalism (Braun & Eklund, 2019), studies into how *analytics* (and metrics) have been appropriated and is being used in newsrooms (Carlson, 2018a;

Zamith, 2018), from the perspective of audience-oriented editors (Ferrer-Conill & Tandoc, 2018), as well as *analytics* companies (Belair-Gagnon & Holton, 2018). We then find studies focusing on the role of *algorithms* for news (Thurman, Moeller, Helberger, & Trilling, 2019; Wallace, 2018), the emergence of *artificial intelligence* in journalism (Broussard, 2015; Stray, 2019), accountability, and, relatedly, *transparency* (Broersma & Harbers, 2018; Diakopoulos, 2015). Down the alphabet, we find this thematic cluster also comprises studies looking into the closely related area of *bots* (De Maeyer & Trudel, 2018; Lokot & Diakopoulos, 2016), *civic tech* and *datafication* (Baack, 2018), *design* (Petre, 2018), *digital* and *web archives* (Severson, 2018; Weber & Napoli, 2018), *digital surveillance* (Thurman, 2018; Waters, 2018), *drone journalism* (Adams, 2019; Holton, Lawson, & Love, 2015), *hacks, hackers, and technologists* (Baack, 2018; Lewis & Usher, 2014; Lewis & Westlund, 2015a), *machine learning* (Broersma & Harbers, 2018; Watanabe, 2018), and many more.

The intersection of journalism and *data* is a common denominator across several keywords and studies published since the inception of the journal *Digital Journalism*. In its inaugural issue we find one article offering rich discussions on the strategies for doing research with Twitter data (Vis, 2013), another focusing on developing methods for automating content analysis of news content (Flaounas et al., 2013), and a third positing a model of journalism incorporating automated journalism, and the study of "the human actors and technological actants performing the work, vis-à-vis the degree to which content and services are platform-agnostic or coupled with specific affordances and logics" (Westlund, 2013, p. 19). In 2013, *Digital Journalism's* inaugural year, the journal also published its first study of analytics and metrics – a case study of how *Al Jazeera English* engaged in activities for tracking and analysing their audience through technological actants (Usher, 2013). That article shows how *Al Jazeera English's* organisational culture shaped the ways in which journalists use analytics and metrics in practice, and how they understand them. In 2014, a pioneering study of data journalism at seven legacy media companies in Sweden identified time and proper training as the main resource constraints for actors to effectively carry out data journalism (Appelgren & Nygren, 2014).

Within the technology thematic cluster, there are three key themes of research: 1) *Data journalism*, 2) *Analytics and metrics*, and 3) *Algorithms and automation*. These three themes show that this interdisciplinary field has turned towards studying the evolving and complex interplay between digital technology and journalism, using different theories, methods, and ways of thinking about these relationships. Next, we highlight some emerging patterns of research in each of these areas in recent years.

3.1 Data journalism

Data journalism works within an epistemological tradition where journalists turn to data as a source for reporting about certain phenomena. It is often seen as a "pure" way of accessing information, but while raw data may give the impression of objectivity, this is an oxymoron (Gitelman, 2013). Many scholars argue that any type of data has its biases and limitations (e.g., Carlson, 2019; S. C. Lewis & Westlund, 2015b; Steensen, 2019). Studies in the field have found that data journalists themselves take on a role of translating technical and abstract knowledge so that their (lay) audience can understand what stories data tell (Boyles & Meyer, 2016). In 2015, *Digital Journalism* published a special issue focusing on the intersection of data and journalism (Lewis, 2015) that has had a formative impact on much subsequent work. As of early February 2020 the five most cited articles from that issue were: "Algorithmic Accountability" (Diakopoulos, 2015) with 141 CrossRef citations, "Clarifying Journalism's Quantitative Turn" with 126 (Coddington, 2015), "The Robotic Reporter" with 85 (Carlson, 2015), "Big Data and Journalism" with 72 (S. C. Lewis & Westlund, 2015b), and "Data-driven Revelation" with 50 (Parasie, 2015).

That special issue features several articles examining how social actors approach data journalism, related for instance to the epistemological concerns of such work (Lewis & Westlund, 2015b), the tensions relating to historical developments regarding data and journalism (Anderson, 2015), and investigative journalism (Parasie, 2015). It also offers insights into the formative approaches to data journalism in Belgium (De Maeyer, Libert, Domingo, Heinderyckx, & Le Cam, 2015).

Scholars and practitioners have envisioned data journalism as enabling new and improved journalistic investigations and reporting practices. There are indeed multiple significant and successful data journalism endeavours that reflect this, such as the reporting on the Panama Papers (Carson & Farhall, 2018). Nevertheless, it remains a challenge for journalists and news organisations trying to integrate data journalism into everyday routines of news reporting, since data journalism requires different sorts of expertise and work flows. Studies continue to show that the relative proportion of data journalists is small and journalists often struggle to access relevant and reliable data to use in their reporting (Appelgren, Lindén, & van Dalen, 2019; Porlezza & Splendore, 2019). In many places, journalists struggle to get hold of data as authorities restrict access, including the ever-present risk of imprisonment or even murder of journalists scrutinising such regimes (Lewis & Nashmi, 2019). Several recent studies show that data journalists at prominent media, including but not limited to *The New York Times* and *The Washington Post*, often use small data sets and seldom carry out advanced data analysis in their everyday news reporting (Anderson & Borges-Rey, 2019; Zamith, 2019). This highlights not only limitations in terms of resources and expertise in newsrooms, but also an adaptation to the envisioned competence of the readership (Anderson & Borges-Rey, 2019) and their interest in participation (Palomo, Teruel, & Blanco-Castilla, 2019). Importantly, it has not only been data journalists participating in producing data journalism, but actors external to the field as well. Studies have found that civic technologists in several continents have important skillsets, which can enable data-based journalism, but also a sense that journalists are unable to do what they should do with data (Cheruiyot, Baack, & Ferrer-Conill, 2019; Cheruiyot & Ferrer-Conill, 2018). Finally, researchers have shown that while attention is now paid to this practice, data journalism is by no means a new journalistic practice, but one that has developed well over time (Anderson, 2018), and one that has emerged in dialogue with technologists (Hermida & Young, 2019; Usher, 2016). Some argue this sub-field has started to mature (Appelgren et al., 2019), and we also find important advancements in data journalism scholarship from the global south, in the form of edited books with contributions by a diverse set of scholars (Mutsvairo, Bebawi, & Borges-Rey, 2019) as well as by scholars and practitioners (Krøvel & Thowsen, 2019).

To sum up briefly, we can see that between 2013 and 2019 there was a burst of scholarly interest in different forms of data journalism. There was also a sense of optimism involved, including in the journalism sector, which envisaged an important appropriation of data journalism in newsrooms. While data journalism scholarship has evolved, and expanded across geographical terrains, a significant body of work has found that, in practice, data journalism requires substantial expertise, access to datasets, and much more. While data journalism can help to enrich journalism, it is likely not a major component in everyday news reporting.

3.2 Analytics and metrics

Analytics refer to the technological infrastructures, systems, and tools for gathering and analysing *metrics* about audiences and their behaviours (Zamith, 2018). Such metrics, which trace data such as page impressions, time spent on pages and sites, completion of article reads, and so on, are being used to guide editorial processes and decisions such as what types of leads journalists prioritise (Chua & Duffy, 2019), and how online editors and algorithms prioritise the exposure different news articles receive (Tandoc, 2019a; Zamith, 2018). Throughout the 2010s there has been a surge in how journalists and newsrooms gravitate towards using analytics for looking at different sorts of editorially oriented metrics. Analytics companies constantly experiment with their products and services to fit the changing demands of news publishers and influence news production practices (Belair-Gagnon & Holton, 2018).

Some would argue that in the past, reporters mainly relied on their gut feeling to make decisions about what stories to pursue and publish (Schultz, 2007). Nowadays there is a wealth of relevant data that can inform news publishers' decision-making, but one should not overlook the many ways reporters of the past were informed about their readers' news consumption. Some news publishers have a long tradition of measuring their audiences by for instance conducting focus group interviews and commissioning surveys and opinion polls, much as researchers do. For example, in Sweden the national newspaper association sponsored the Newspaper Research Programme at the University of Gothenburg from 1979 to 2011, funding studies into news consumption and attitudes. This contributed significantly to the establishment of a research institute that conducts annual cross-sectional surveys, similarly to how the Reuters Institute for the Study of Journalism has later built the comparative survey project with much funding coming from Google, which has renewed sponsorship into the 2020s. By comparison, and telling for the publisher and platform industries, funding from the national newspaper association ended in 2011 in part because of the worsening financial situation for newspaper companies, and in part because of the growth in options for analysing audiences.

At the same time, news publishers trying to find ways of securing readers and revenue were also subscribing to services from industry data providers like ComScore and Kantar, which gave them data reflecting the behaviours and attitudes of their audiences. These companies also began to offer analytics that could fetch and put on display data about the behavioural digital footprints people were leaving behind as they used the web to navigate to and from news articles. For instance, when analysing mobile media throughout 2008–2010, Swedish journalists, technologists, and business people combined Kantar data with services like Google Analytics to analyse trace data about page impressions, time spent, and audience engagement in comment fields, alongside metrics from Apple about the number of app installs. This allowed them to evaluate how their native mobile news app was performing (Westlund, 2011). Throughout the 2010s, on top of using industry data from panels and such for their business intelligence, the journalism sector has also increased its emphasis on the use of analytics and metrics. Companies like Kantar have developed services where they combine different data, such as survey data and metrics from websites.

Research into how newsrooms approached analytics and metrics began to emerge early in the 2010s. At the beginning of the decade, pioneering research about developments in the US were published by scholars based either in the US (C. W. Anderson, 2011a, 2011c; Lee, Lewis, & Powers, 2014) or Singapore (Tandoc, 2014). There was also early contributions into this area coming from Sweden (Karlsson & Clerwall, 2013). While, as noted earlier, *Digital Journalism* published a pioneering study into how *Al Jazeera* uses analytics and metrics in its first year (Usher, 2013), it was another two years before a second article on this topic was published in the journal. In this article, Tandoc and Thomas (2015) raised three concerns: 1) viewing the audience as disaggregated segments, 2) failing to distinguish between interest and public interest, and 3) arguing against journalistic autonomy and romanticising the audience. There is clearly a strong link to business activities when it comes to developing technological actants with the purpose of measuring and analysing audiences. In their study on so-called engineering technologies, Slaček Brlek, Smrke, and Vobič (2017) discuss that newsrooms had an inferior role compared to the business people in defining and implementing goals for these technologies. To continue, in Dwyer and Martin's (2017) article on news sharing and social media analytics, the authors discuss in a critical fashion how news media have become dependent on such analytics and how this can influence news diversity. Another article draws on Bourdieu's field theory to position journalism as a field in which audience analytics is a trend and driving force with implications for journalism (Q. Wang, 2018).

Belair-Gagnon and Holton (2018) offer insight into how representatives for web analytics companies see their role and function in news production. They conclude that web analytics companies do not take responsibility as journalists, and largely work towards continuous developments of their analytics through experimentation. Moreover, based on substantial ethnographic work at an analytics start-up, Petre (2018) finds that they engineer and design their analytics to match editorial routines and judgments, while turning down the prevalence of managerial influence. Another ethnographic study of a company specialised in global audience engagement services finds that there is no agreed-upon standard for audience engagement and therefore the company struggles to quantify its value proposition (Nelson, 2018). These articles were part of a 2018 special issue in *Digital Journalism* focusing on what the guest editor refers to as *measurable* journalisms, consisting of eight diverse dimensions (Carlson, 2018a, p. 409).

This special issue also included studies reporting on how audience-oriented editors engage with the metrics produced by analytics in different activities geared towards stimulating audience engagement (Ferrer-Conill & Tandoc, 2018). A year later a cross-cultural study into the use of analytics and metrics in Zimbabwean, Kenyan, and South African newsrooms was published, exemplifying the changing approaches to how news organisations analyse and interact with their audiences. All in all, the authors argue that these newsrooms engage in so-called analytics-driven journalism (Moyo, Mare, & Matsilele, 2019).

Studies are also signaling how journalists and audience-oriented editors often have to work with metrics produced by third-party analytics companies, such as Google (Analytics), Facebook (CrowdTangle), Chartbeat, etc. Some of these offer unique metrics, and there are different advantages and disadvantages to them. Journalists, editors, and others in the newsroom are naturally interested in knowing as much as possible as part of their newswork, and thus would want to be able to combine analytics that gather metrics from their proprietary platforms with analytics like CrowdTangle to study audience engagement on Facebook. Powers (2018) discusses this, examining how journalists across a diverse set of news organisations define, measure, and discuss the potential impact of metrics on their journalistic work. Some turn to measures focusing on whether the published news has entered public discourse, public policy, or public awareness, while others simply rely on the metrics coming from audience analytics companies. In another case study, Blanchett Neheli (2018) found the newsroom is very much oriented to traffic-based metrics, which may negatively affect their ability to maintain journalistic standards. A group of American scholars selected a couple of common metrics and surveyed US newsworkers about how useful they found these to be. They concluded that the metrics were most useful for enacting the newsworkers' consumer role orientation (Belair-Gagnon, Zamith, & Holton, 2020).

Analytics and metrics have certainly gained prominence in many contemporary newsrooms and have changed newswork and routines for many journalists. It is an important area of research in digital journalism studies, and there are many more publications in other journals also addressing it, not to mention a recent book which has charted how this line of research is maturing, showing the significance of work in this field in a holistic way for the first time (Tandoc, 2019a). Throughout the 2010s there were multiple qualitative studies raising questions concerning whether analytics and metrics influence editorial judgment. By the end of the last decade, the answer in many cases was "yes". In this context we should recall that such questions may well generate responses guided by normativity and role perceptions, and reflect scenarios where journalists do not want to admit to how their news judgment might be influenced by metrics about their audiences' behaviours and needs. We should also bear in mind that most studies are conducted in a Western context, making the comparative study of analytics-driven journalism in African countries all the more important for breaking from that limited scope (Moyo et al., 2019). It is worth noting that, when looking beyond *Digital Journalism*, we find additional journal publications into analytics in the global south. One article focused on how correspondent in sub-Saharan Africa, mainly Nairobi and Lagos, diverge substantially in their approaches to analytics and metrics (Bunce, 2015), and another revealed how metricsare used by web and traffic managers in Kenyan newsrooms. Also several studies into analytics and metrics have been carried out in Singapore (Duffy, Tandoc, & Ling, 2018), South Korea (Yang, 2016), the Philippines (David, Tandoc, & Katigbak, 2019), as well as mainland China (Zhu et al., 2019).

Going into the 2020s, the journalism sector will likely work more with their news organisations' proprietary platforms, and the analytics and metrics associated with them. With many news publishers now getting most of their revenues from readers rather than from advertisers, there must be a shift: metrics data does not derive its main importance in relation to advertisers and reach, but rather in providing insights that journalists, editors, and other news workers can use when they make editorial judgments, personalise news distribution, and so forth. While much is known about how analytics and metrics shape news production and content, less is known about how individual journalists are affected and navigate this. Ultimately, scholars should also advance more research into all eight dimensions of measurable journalism, including the material aspects of analytics (and the innovations taking place in this realm) and how this potentially assists the economic aspects, but especially reader revenue.

3.3 Algorithms and automation

Algorithms are everywhere and they have lots of power. However, and as Bucher (2017a) argues, they do not have instincts and are not only technical, but also cultural, economic, social, and political. From 2013 to 2015 there were only a handful of articles in *Digital Journalism* analysing or discussing the role of algorithms and automation per se. These included a model of journalism focusing on human-machine interaction referenced above (Westlund, 2013), and an article presenting the testing of a prototype software system that uses artificial intelligence to assist reporters in processing large amounts of data and detecting leads for investigative journalism (Broussard, 2015). The remaining articles were published in a special issue focusing on journalism and big data (Lewis & Westlund, 2015). One article in this issue advanced understandings of automated journalism through a study of such practices at Narrative Science, a tech company using artificial intelligence (AI) to convert data into narratives that are easy to understand (Carlson, 2015), while another analysed how computational journalism influenced the creation and dissemination of crime news at *The Los Angeles Times* and their pioneering "Homicide Report" project (Young & Hermida, 2015). The special issue also featured an article focusing on algorithmic accountability, and the power structures, biases, and influences associated with employing algorithms in journalism (Diakopoulos, 2015). To date (early 2020), this is the most cited article of all time in *Digital Journalism*. In 2016, Diakopoulos contributed further to this area of research in a coauthored article focusing on news bots in social media – those accounts that are not managed by social actors but technological actants – which are automated to participate in news distribution (Lokot & Diakopoulos, 2016).

As research in this area developed, a focus on efficacy and ethics became salient. Scholars have studied the distinct nature of technology by assessing more specifically technological actants. One article looked at how these issues addressed the case of technological actants developed to have a "nose for news". In this article, the authors critically examined the SocialSensor application developed in a EU project, finding that while it indeed enabled sourcing and verification through social media, it also reflected certain biases, such as towards using men as sources (Thurman et al., 2016). Further, in a mapping of current qualifications of technological actants for algorithmic selection and production of news texts through natural language generation, Dörr (2016) showed that while there are few companies on the market, the technologies as they stand are "good enough" to be used. However, another study finds that journalists with personal experiences of working with software for automated journalism raised concerns about sourcing and capacity to identify news stories (Thurman, Dörr, & Kunert, 2017). Both of these studies discuss how the social actors interviewed, in journalism and at software companies for automation respectively, expect automated journalism to expand further. As a counter-narrative to the dominant discourse around automation, Lindén (2017) argued that we should ask, "Why are there still so many jobs in journalism after decades of newsroom automation?"

Scholars of digital journalism studies have continued to gear their efforts towards this area of algorithms and automation. It is an expanding field marked by more heterogeneity as emerging developments are studied. *Digital Journalism* has published empirical studies on how social actors assess changing structures pushing automation forward, but also on the importance of journalists' agency, their attitudes and skillsets (Wu, Tandoc, & Salmon, 2019). Other studies focus on attribution regimes and bylines in automated journalism (Montal & Reich, 2017), and the challenges for adopting and communicating algorithmic transparency (Bodó, 2019). One experimental study found that people do not expect human-written news to be more credible, and prefer automated news when it comes to credibility (Haim & Graefe, 2017) whereas another experimental study found that audiences assess news produced by technological actants as less credible than news produced by (human) journalists (Waddell, 2018). A different line of research deals with how algorithms and code are utilised to prioritise the exposure and distribution of news for different platforms and channels (Weber & Kosterich, 2018), and also algorithmic selection guided by individual news consumption routines. A cross-cultural survey study (26 countries) found that citizens favour algorithmic selection compared to editorial curation by social actors (Thurman, Moeller, et al., 2019).

The research into algorithms and automation in news was drawn together in 2019, when a special issue on this theme was guest edited by Thurman, Lewis, and Kunert (2019). The editors discuss how the articles in the special issue advance earlier research focusing on algorithms and automation in news, and how this can help to develop digital journalism by taking a broader approach to understanding the technologies involved, discussing their diverse uses as well as the challenges involved for practice and values in utilising AI. This issue highlights that there are certainly great challenges for using AI in investigative journalism, restricted by factors such as the affordances of technological actants, costs, access to data, accuracy standards, and so forth (Stray, 2019). It also foregrounds a challenge concerning the tension between automated and human-produced journalism, perhaps most notably when it comes to ideals such as autonomy, objectivity, and public service (Milosavljević & Vobič, 2019). Objectivity, or more specifically an idea of a so-called mechanical objectivity, that comes with the discourse of automation, however, also warrants critique. Carlson (2019) argues this discourse risks replicating an argument that technology can offer more objective representations than humans can.

Further in this issue, we gain insights into how the BBC has set in motion a series of news bots operating on their website as well as third-party platforms not owned or controlled by them, with the goal of reaching audiences they struggle to reach via their proprietary platforms (Jones & Jones, 2019). A study of ABC's news bot, in the same issue, finds that both journalists and the public express an appreciation for the forms of news delivery it enables, and discusses concerns relating to control over data and how ABC depends on third-party platforms (Ford & Hutchinson, 2019). This highlights differing priorities for different companies involved in these processes. As Bodó (2019) reports, news publishers work with personalisation with goals such as showing relevant news content and selling subscriptions, whereas platform companies such as Facebook strive towards substantial engagement on their platform so they can monetise attention through advertisements. Extending this, Helberger (2019) offers an interdisciplinary conceptual framework for news recommenders tailored to different democratic models. On a related note, other articles have also made theoretical advances in the journal, bringing the field of human-machine communication into dialogue with digital journalism studies for the study of technological actants as active message sources and not only mediators of communication (Lewis, Guzman, & Schmidt, 2019).

Going into the 2020s, there are many reasons to suggest algorithms and automation will become increasingly intertwined with the production and distribution of news. The accuracy of automated journalism depends on the quality of the data it builds on, as well as the level of complexity inherent in the issues and events that technological actants are to create news and make truth claims about. The type of automated journalism evident in the 2010s involved mainly reporting on topics and events that are relatively easy areas for journalists and technologists to develop automated journalism for, such as fiscal reports and sports journalism. They typically develop predefined algorithms based on news values, which are matched with the dataset, generating news stories fed to news distribution platforms via an interconnected content management system.

There are massive investments being made in AI. However, while there is currently a great deal of buzz about the potential of AI, we must once again be cautious and critical about this future, rather than falling into traps of thinking that this is the next technology that will save journalism. Most investments in AI, for instance, can be traced to Asia and more specifically to China. A power concentration in AI capacity can become problematic if newsrooms around the world become overly dependent on AI services provided by companies in specific countries. In extension of this, the Chinese authorities could gain influence over significant data and automated news flows taking place across the world.

Editorial-facing innovation in AI in the news industries will depend, however, on the leaps taken by the industry as a whole. Appropriating AI into news reporting raises key questions of accountability and libel (S. C. Lewis, Sanders, & Carmody, 2019; S. C. Lewis & Westlund, 2016). News publishers are responsible for the news they publish, and it can become very problematic if they use AI technology to report misinformation, especially if the ownership of such non-proprietary technology is associated with political or economic interests.

Already today news publishers and journalists could take advantage of AI by making use of advanced tools for analysing open-source Earth data provided by Copernicus (EU funded) and NASA. This data is accessible, overcoming a main problem in data journalism, although the analysis of data still requires certain expertise (Appelgren et al., 2019), while the combination of data and images/videos allows for major truth claims, with an implied mechanical objectivity (Carlson, 2019) because they represent visual representations of reality, and a sense of seeing things how they are. Obviously, those with ill intents can easily manipulate images and videos. Nevertheless, recent research has revealed how reporters successfully have used satellite images in investigative journalism (Seo, 2020). Moving towards using such online repositories of satellite images, big data, and visually oriented user interfaces can help journalists advance reporting on complex and urgently important matters such as climate change, and possibly offer credible reporting that even climate change deniers will embrace. Clearly, this also open doors for avenues digital journalism studies scholars have hardly yet explored.

3.4 Concluding discussion

This chapter has dealt with three specific areas of research that are central components of the technology thematic cluster in *Digital Journalism*: data journalism, analytics and metrics, and algorithms, automation, and news. Our assessment demonstrates how research into journalism and technology has mainly focused on how journalism changes in relation to data and algorithms, with a significant amount of research into how data (analytics and metrics) drives journalism, how data (datasets, visualisations etc.) becomes part of journalistic practice, and also how algorithms are used for producing and distributing news.

We would like to point to some patterns from our assessment in light of the so-called 4 A's: social actors, technological actants, audiences, and activities (S. C. Lewis & Westlund, 2015a). We find that relatively few studies have focused on the technologies per se, and the agency inscribed into the technological actant (exceptions include Diakopoulos, 2015 and Helberger, 2019). Scholars have typically studied either how social actors approach emerging technologies, such as journalists appropriating analytics in their daily practice, or they have studied audience attitudes to automated journalism or personalised news recommenders. While it is very challenging and time-consuming to adopt holistic approaches to the study of actors, actants, and audiences, the stream of more focused studies on only one of the A's means that different studies must be conjoined to attain a broader view. More holistic approaches are possible when journals commission special issues. This is the case with some of the research areas discussed in this chapter, such as the *Digital Journalism* special issues into analytics and metrics (Carlson, 2018a) and data journalism (Appelgren et al., 2019) as well as algorithms and automation (Thurman, Lewis, et al., 2019).

Let us end this chapter by discussing the intersection of technology and *audiences*. The research we have reviewed and discussed would not by tradition fall into a classification of audience research. However, an underlying driving force for the research developed on analytics and metrics has to do with how analytics as a form of technological actant can be developed and used for assessing behavioural patterns among audiences and, in turn, how they are diffused into routines of news work. Researchers can easily build on this line of research to study the analytics infrastructures itself, as well as turning their attention to the metrics themselves. As for research into data journalism, the focus generally lies with social actors and their newswork. As with the potential opportunities in analytics research, some scholars have surfaced audience-oriented questions relating to their interest in participation (Palomo et al., 2019) and their competences (Anderson & Borges-Rey, 2019). Similarly, the research into automation and algorithms has raised important questions about how audiences may be approached through news recommender systems depending on different democratic models (Helberger, 2019). Associated with such developments, we find audience-oriented research studying attitudes to news personalisation (Bodó, Helberger, Eskens, & Möller, 2019), and the role of humans and algorithms in selecting the news that is exposed (Thurman, Moeller, et al., 2019). In advancing this argument, Guzman (2019, p. 1187) makes a call for researchers to further mobilise efforts for the study of audiences in relation to technologies of automation such as news recommenders and chatbots. In this context, we envision further research into what Bucher (2017b) refers to as algorithmic imaginary among citizens would be worthwhile to advance knowledge into how citizens imagine algorithms operate with news among publishers and platforms. As we move into the 2020s, digital journalism studies will continue to advance research into technology, and will likely include audience-oriented research into algorithms, news recommenders, chatbots, and algorithms, among other topics.

4 The platforms

Distributions and devices
in digital journalism

For much of the 20th century, legacy news media reached mass audiences via printed newspapers or radio or television broadcasting. Legacy news media companies have, by tradition, owned and controlled their means of distribution. The printing press has constituted a backbone in newspaper companies, and frequency licences and news broadcasting studios have been central to broadcasting companies. With the World Wide Web news publishers extended their news distribution by way of setting up proprietary news sites, and eventually also turning to other devices such as smartphones and tablets. However, around 2007 and 2008 news publishers started losing control over how news was distributed, and became increasingly dependent on non-proprietary platforms. Such platforms were gaining significance for the ways people were accessing the news. There was a massive orientation towards creating native mobile applications for smartphones. News publishers essentially made their news accessible for mobile devices (Westlund, 2013) and the·public has since increasingly moved towards mobile news consumption (Nelson & Lei, 2018; Newman et al., 2019; Westlund & Färdigh, 2015).

For those news publishers who did move to mobile apps for the iPhone, they had to contemplate the requirements defined by Apple, including sharing 30 percent of all revenues with them. Using Apple devices as platforms also meant that news companies would feed Apple with metrics about news consumption. News publishers joined each other in herd behaviour under mantras such as being innovative, and that they were developing a presence in the mobile "ecosystems" where their (younger) users were. With mobile ecosystems we refer to the mobile interfaces established and largely facilitated by Apple and Android, enabling actors to develop native mobile applications deemed to fit with user-friendliness and usability for smartphones (Goggin, 2009, 2020; Gómez-Barroso et al., 2010). News publishers mobilised efforts for developing their brand and their content within such mobile ecosystems. At the same time, news publishers embarked on a journey where they became increasingly dependent on third parties for their distribution, data, revenues, and so on. We would like to clarify that this was not entirely new. The so-called "walled gardens" for mobile devices (sites/portals for mobile devices controlled by telecom operators), such as by DoCoMo in Japan and Telia in Sweden, by the turn of the millennium were indeed precursors with similarities. However, with the iPhone and the App Store, this gained widespread momentum (Westlund, 2011, 2012). Such dependence on third parties certainly did not stop at mobile ecosystems but extended to platform companies, most notably Facebook, Google, and Twitter in Western democracies. From a survey with Nordic news media managers, we learn that the opportunities the managers saw as most important were mobile news (73 percent), social media (68 percent), and tablets (65 percent) (Stone, Nel, & Wilberg, 2010).

Throughout the 2010s there has been enormous activity in the journalism sector associated with the developments of mobile ecosystems and global platforms. The activities of companies like Apple, Facebook, and Google have a lot of visibility and are closely followed by the media and other companies, and they oftentimes gain a prominent place at various work places as well as in the everyday lives of citizens. Returning to our analytical framework introduced in chapter 2, section 2.2, we see that not only is there issue visibility and innovation bias at play, but also practical addressability in terms of research designs. Correspondingly, a wealth of research has emerged in digital journalism studies focusing on platforms and digital devices. Much of this research has been marked by optimism and how news publishers, journalists, and users can explore the emerging opportunities, albeit that there are also some studies focusing on challenges and problems arising concerning dependence, loss of revenues, and privacy.

This chapter focuses on two main areas of research into the *platforms* thematic cluster: 1) *Digital journalism and platforms*, and 2) *Digital journalism and digital devices*. The first area aligns with the emerging and increasingly common approach referring to platforms as digital intermediaries between different stakeholders in communication, entertainment, news distribution, and so forth. The second area focuses on how digital devices such as desktops and smartphones (and potentially also tablets, smart watches, smart TVs, screens in cars, and others-), are developed and appropriated in the context of the production, distribution, and consumption of news. We link the research discussed to research on *audience*, the third biggest thematic cluster.

4.1 Digital journalism and platforms

Journalism, and digital journalism, has evolved in parallel and also sometimes in tandem with the developments of the World Wide Web and platforms (Burgess & Hurcombe, 2019). There are many digital platforms, including but not limited to Facebook, WhatsApp, Instagram, Twitter, WeChat, Telegram, Snapchat, Google, and Amazon. In this review of research on platforms, we refer to a platforms as "a digital infrastructure with affordances offering diverse kinds of information and communication, as well as opportunities to produce, publish and engage with content" (Ekström & Westlund, 2019b, p. 259).

This section features two sub-sections, each referring to different facets in digital journalism and digital journalism studies: 1) *building platform presence*, and 2) *platform counterbalancing*. Building platform presence is a facet marked by a rather optimistic approach to platforms (especially social media platforms) in both industry and research, oftentimes normatively building on the assumption that news publishers and journalists should build a platform presence by improving their expertise, by normalising different social media into their routines, by developing social media policies, by producing unique content for social media or customising content they already have, by striving towards expanding eyeballs via social media traffic, or by appropriating analytics tools provided by platform companies (e.g., Google, Facebook, CrowdTangle, etc.). The list goes on. The second facet, *platform counterbalancing*, is associated with publishers seeking to balance their relationship with, and dependence on, platforms that are non-proprietary to them. Such efforts surface in different ways, for example when publishers are more cautious about giving news content away for free, or even producing unique news content for platform companies. We borrow the concept of platform counterbalancing from Chua and Westlund (2019), who posited it based on their longitudinal study of two Singaporean news publishers shifting their approach to platform companies over time. Please note that we present these facets as distinct from each other (in practice and in research) for the sake of simplicity and clarity. These facets are not in a binary relationship, and thus a publisher can simultaneously work on building platform presence in some ways, and engage in platform counterbalancing on other ends.

4.1.1 Building platform presence

Let us rewind to the end of the first decade of the 2000s, when YouTube was a new phenomenon showing tremendous growth, when Apple launched the iPhone and App Store, when Facebook rolled out and got more international traction for its platform, and when Twitter spurred a rapid growth in micro-blogging. All of these platform innovations were receiving a good deal of attention from the public, from the media, and also from companies. News publishers were, metaphorically speaking, on a "mobile media train" about to leave the "platform", a train which they needed to be quick to catch if they were to maintain their relevance in the emerging age of mobile media and news. News publishers have been keen to build a presence on Apple and Android platforms for mobile news, for strategic reasons of reaching out to specific segments as well as to gain symbolic recognition (Westlund, 2011, 2014). Similar logics seem to have been in play when it comes to how journalists and news publishers have approached social media platforms. They either needed to join the social media bandwagon, or be viewed as a laggard that failed to keep up with contemporary trends and developments. Such mechanisms of pro-innovation and pro-platforms have spurred tremendous growth, as they collectively have built a self-fulfilling prophecy in which social media presence has been taken for granted to be desirable. Publishers have approached platforms with ambitions towards maintaining a broad user base, and attracting more traffic, which potentially generates eyeballs that drive advertising revenues. Publishers have thus allowed third-party actors, who own and control commercial platforms non-proprietary to them, to host their news content and facilitate participation around it.

Several reviews and books have witnessed how digital journalism scholars have been eager to follow in the footsteps of the journalism sector and how publishers have built platform presence. Studies have been developed into how news publishers and journalists have been exploring, appropriating, and normalising social media platforms into their news work (Eldridge II & Franklin, 2019; Franklin & Eldridge II, 2017; Steensen et al., 2019; Witschge, Anderson, Domingo., & Hermida, 2016b). Recent literature reviews attest to the intersection of journalism and social media being a burgeoning area of research, encompassing thousands of journal articles over the past decade (Lewis & Molyneux, 2018; Segado-Boj, 2020). A 2017 report from the Tow Center for Digital Journalism discussed how silicon valley has reengineered the news industry, essentially fostering a so-called platform press that operates much in tandem with platform companies (Bell & Owen, 2017). Many have studied how news publishers and journalists have reconfigured what they do, recalibrating their expertise and routines in order to develop their social media presence. This extends not only to commercial news media, but also to public service broadcasters such as SVT, NRK, and DR in Scandinavia, and the BBC in the UK. In her case study of social media at the BBC, Belair-Gagnon (2015) shows how social media surface as emerging media, which the newsroom and its journalists experimented with and gradually normalised, demonstrating that management outlines formal expectations for their journalists to cross-publish and promote their news materials on social media. Hermida (2010) discusses how Twitter and micro-blogging have given birth to a new form of journalism that gives precedence to instant dissemination of brief fragments of information. He posits ambient journalism as a concept referring to how such journalism, via social media, enables citizens to develop a sort of awareness system.

Much of digital journalism studies scholarship on platforms has been marked by three important characteristics: 1) it has predominantly focused on social media platforms, and less on search engine platforms or mobile platforms provided by Android and Apple; 2) scholars have mainly studied social media platforms used in Western contexts; and 3) there are particularly many studies of Twitter. Scholars have oftentimes conducted research focusing on Twitter because it is a more public platform for which data is relatively easily accessible, for example by using Twittonomy to access and analyse patterns, compared to platforms such as Facebook that has become increasingly unavailable after the previously mentioned Cambridge Analytica case (Burgess & Hurcombe, 2019; Venturini & Rogers, 2019). Moreover, following the implementation of GDPR regulation there are substantial restrictions to API data resulting in less data being available for analytics companies as well as researchers (Bruns et al., 2018). Some of the research articles that have been published in *Digital Journalism* have used data that would not be possible to access with their current data policies (Bechmann & Nielbo, 2018).

In the following, we will look more in detail at the research published in *Digital Journalism* related to specific platforms: Twitter, Facebook, WhatsApp, Google, and more.

Twitter

Studies on Twitter and journalism include how Twitter is used for breaking news (Bennett, 2016; Shermak, 2018; Thurman & Walters, 2013; Verweij & Van Noort, 2014; Vis, 2013), for constructing professional identities, the branding and promotion of news (Brems, Temmerman, Graham, & Broersma, 2017; Molyneux & Holton, 2015; Olausson, 2017; F. M. Russell, 2019), agenda setting and influence (Kapidzic, Neuberger, Stieglitz, & Mirbabaie, 2019; F. M. Russell, 2019), as well as how journalists tweet about politics, or use politicians' tweets about politics (Metag & Rauchfleisch, 2017; Mourão, Diehl, & Vasudevan, 2016).

Let us discuss in brief a few among several examples. Digital journalism scholars have focused on *who* the journalists using Twitter are, (Djerf-Pierre et al., 2016; Hanusch & Nölleke, 2019; Hedman, 2015; Willnat & Weaver, 2018). There are also studies of the ways that journalists/news media, public actors, and private actors interact with each other via Twitter. Publishers maintain an important role whereas private actors have influence mostly during crisis situations (Kapidzic et al., 2019). In another study into the intersection of journalism and crisis situations, where the study of hyperlinks on Twitter was combined with other methods, the authors concluded that societal resilience was established among Norwegians (Steensen & Eide, 2019). Another article analysed a random sample of 1.8 billion tweets and found that publishers only contribute to a fraction of all Twitter activity, but have a more pronounced position when it comes to countries of conflict (Malik & Pfeffer, 2016). There are also other studies into *how* news publishers use official accounts for promotion and interactivity (F. M. Russell, 2019), as well as in live sports journalism, for which analysis, opinion, visual content, and entertainment generated more likes and retweets than play-by-play results (Shermak, 2018), and how journalists use Twitter for photojournalism and more personalised reporting connected to emotions (Pantti, 2019). In this context it is worth paying attention to a UK study of how reporters use Twitter for personalised (but not personal) reporting, to brand themselves (Canter, 2015).

This territory of digital journalism studies also features scholarship advancing how Twitter can be used in the creation of an automated Twitter account that sends tweets about the writings of Franklin Ford, who was known to think about the future of the news (De Maeyer & Trudel, 2018). Moreover, scholars have turned to the Twittersphere in order to study and analyse how the public tweet about specific phenomena, such as "data-driven journalism" (X. Zhang, 2018). In another original contribution analysing Black Twitter, the black public sphere and media witnessing are triangulated in a discussion of how scholars can approach sousveillance via Twitter using mobile devices (Richardson, 2017).

Throughout the 2010s journalists have learnt how to turn to social media for online sourcing, including but not limited to Twitter. Sourcing via social media potentially opens the gateway for voicing a much broader and heterogenic public in journalism. However, in practice this does not necessarily mean that citizens are featured in stories, as elite groups are overrepresented on Twitter and also because journalists largely rely on predefined networks of sources (Ekström & Westlund, 2019a). A comprehensive study of Twitter interactions in relation to the Germanwings accident showed that few citizens functioned as eyewitnesses, but they did act as watchdogs of the watchdogs when communicating about the shortcomings in news reporting (Masip, Ruiz, & Suau, 2019). Another study indicates practices oriented towards protection of online sources cannot be taken for granted (Henrichsen, 2019).

Relatively few scholars have simultaneously studied patterns regarding how journalism interrelates with both Twitter and Facebook. Exceptions here include a study on how one major news publisher, in Germany, the UK, and the US respectively, has increased social media sourcing from

Twitter and Facebook over time (von Nordheim, Boczek, & Koppers, 2018); another study finding that social media citizen sourcing remains relatively unusual (Vliegenthart & Boukes, 2018); and a study showing that men consistently were cited as sources from Twitter and Facebook twice as much (Mitchelstein, Andelsman, & Boczkowski, 2019). Other examples of articles reporting on multiple social media platforms include an analysis of a specific issue (the Ice Bucket Challenge) finding that articles with emotional appeals were most likely to be shared on these platforms (Kilgo, Lough, & Riedl, 2020), as well as an interview-based Australian study focusing on how sport organisations have turned to Twitter, Facebook, and other social media to communicate with their own strategic frames, resulting in news publishers having less power in what was once a more symbiotic relationship (Sherwood, Nicholson, & Marjoribanks, 2017).

Facebook and WhatsApp

Concerning Facebook, digital journalism studies includes studies assessing for example how news publishers have developed formats (headline, lead, and picture) for presenting their news materials on Facebook (Hågvar, 2019; Welbers & Opgenhaffen, 2019), practices for such distribution (Ekström & Westlund, 2019b), and how (an earlier version of) the Facebook algorithm influenced news exposure (Bechmann & Nielbo, 2018). Several studies into Facebook and journalism deal with how audiences relate to news on the platform. Cross-cultural survey research has been used for studies into how citizens bypass the news media to follow politicians via social media (Fisher, Culloty, Lee, & Park, 2019). Multi-method research from Sweden involving a combination of representative survey data and interviews with teenagers shows that social media news-accessing is explained by age, interest in news, and habits for online news consumption, and also that the young take for granted that they will become informed (Bergström & Jervelycke Belfrage, 2018). One study used networked analysis and media experience for an analysis of news consumption patterns in Norway, and found a significant audience overlap when it comes to Facebook and online news from local and regional news publishers (Olsen, 2019). There are also studies into how citizens are sharing news articles on Facebook (Almgren, 2017), as well as engagement among those stumbling across news shared on Facebook (Kümpel, 2019). A focus group study reports how people share news with each other in private social media groups (Facebook and WhatsApp), based on their belonging to location-based, work-related, or leisure-oriented communities (Swart, Peters, & Broersma, 2019).

Several recent studies have focused on how WhatsApp is used for journalism and news, especially in non-Western countries where this platform is more popular. A study conducted in the context of the 2017 Chilean elections showed that sharing and discussing news on WhatsApp was equally popular across different social groups (Valenzuela, Bachmann, & Bargsted, 2019), while a study of Rwandan journalists shed light on how they use WhatsApp to generate new ideas for stories, for online sourcing and communication with audiences, for collaboration with other journalists, and for news distribution (McIntyre & Sobel, 2019). Another study focused on how German publishers have approached WhatsApp when it comes to technological change (distribution) and relational change (engagement), concluding that there are various approaches, some which include pushing unique news content for WhatsApp (Boczek & Koppers, 2020).

YouTube, Google, Instagram, and more

Digital journalism studies also features important studies that investigate the role and/or practices related to YouTube, Instagram, Google, and other platforms. Let us briefly discuss a few examples. By assessing the most viewed videos on the YouTube channels run by four major news companies (the *Guardian*, *The New York Times*, *Washington Post*, and *Wall Street Journal*), one study concluded that the news videos going viral often focus on positive news, while having less social significance (Al-Rawi, 2019). Another study concluded that journalistic videos on YouTube came with calls for political, economic, and social/lifestyle actions, and that audiences developed comments about political and social accountability (Djerf-Pierre, Lindgren, & Budinski, 2019). Other research into YouTube has also focused on news video consumption (Kalogeropoulos, 2018), and on hostility and civility in comments (Ksiazek, Peer, & Zivic, 2015).

Only a few articles in *Digital Journalism* have focused on Instagram. One study has reported on how Instagram users, acting as citizen photojournalists, posted informative images from the Charlie Hebdo incident (Al Nashmi, 2018). Another looked into how citizen- and professional photojournalists use Instagram in their performative work, and how they communicate either their professionalism or amateurish authenticity via their photos and communication (Borges-Rey, 2015). One article reported on China and emerging business models for news start-ups, in a country where several of the platform companies so popular in the West are forbidden, where instead the Chinese use Weibo and WeChat. Some start-ups are content-oriented, whereas others are clearly focusing on building a platform presence, what the author refers to as platform-oriented (S. I. Zhang, 2019). There is more research into these platforms with relevance for digital journalism studies, but published in other journals, such as *Asian Journal of Communication* (Cui & Lin, 2015). As 2020 began, there was a call for more research into studying and comparing social-technical characteristics and implications across diverse platforms such as WhatsApp and WeChat (Goggin, 2020).

Now let us turn to the intersection of journalism studies and Google. The difficulties in studying this intersection presumably makes one important reason there are relatively few studies, and such difficulties are brought to light in a method article assessing the role of endogenous factors (like keywords, language settings, clicks, and geo-location) as well as exogenous factors (experimentation and randomisation), suggesting scholars should study real-world participants or constructed research profiles (Ørmen, 2016). Researchers have furthermore studied how personalisation (explicit and implicit) affects the source and content diversity of Google News, leading them to discard the filter bubble hypothesis (Haim, Graefe, & Brosius, 2018). Also Puschmann (2019) has questioned the validity of the filter bubble concept, following his study of Google News and Google Search in conjunction with the German general elections in 2017. A third study, drawing on data from four countries (UK, US, Germany, Spain), analyses news repertoires among users and non-users of search engines for news (Fletcher & Nielsen, 2018). The findings question hypotheses about echo chambers and filter bubbles because those who use search engines for news are also more likely to access news from more diverse sources.

4.1.2 Platform counterbalancing

This section steps away from building a platform presence and focuses on "opportunities" with platforms. Consider for a moment that the journalism sector (and other sectors) has bought into the idea that it must engage in search engine optimisation (SEO) and social media optimisation (SMO). By engaging in SEO and SMO, news publishers essentially customise or adapt their content, communication, and distribution in ways that fit with the preferences of the platform companies and their algorithms. Ultimately, news publishers have provided platform companies with content for their platforms, sometimes even content optimised for them. This essentially means that the news, produced by commercial as well as public service news publishers, functions as a catalyst for audience engagement on platforms non-proprietary to the news publishers (see for instance Westlund & Ekström, 2018). This also means that when accessing the news, audiences leave digital footprints that platform companies can capitalise on. Platform companies analyse these digital footprints in close detail as they feed their advertising infrastructures and developments of existing and new services. Every now and then it becomes publicly known that platform companies have collected and/or shared sensitive data in ways not expected, as with the Cambridge Analytica case discussed in chapter 1.

In their review essay on social media research related to journalism, Lewis and Molyneux (2018) bring forth and scrutinise what they refer to as three faulty assumptions: 1) that social media would be a net positive; 2) that social media reflects reality; and 3) that social media matters over and above other factors. The authors intentionally seek to advance provocations, identify blind spots, and critically reflect on scholarship. This review article was featured in a special issue focusing on "News and Participation through and beyond Proprietary Platforms in an Age of Social Media", for which the guest editors write:

> Journalism studies, more specifically, should critically assess the political economy of platform companies in relation to the news media. This relates to how the news media are seeking to enable vis-à-vis disable platform companies in maintaining a dominant role for news distribution and public participation. Many news media have struggled to enable and curate positive forms of participation. After years of giving away news content to social media platforms, as well as enabling the public to engage with the news via non-proprietary platforms, some news organizations have started questioning the long-term consequences of doing so.
>
> (Westlund & Ekström, 2018, p. 8)

In essence, throughout the 2010s news publishers have become dependent on platforms non-proprietary to them for exposure and participation, yet have attracted limited revenues in such ways (Kleis Nielsen & Ganter, 2018; Myllylahti, 2018; Westlund & Ekström, 2018), with an overall dislocation of news journalism taking place in which news publishers may well engage in epistemic practices for social media platforms (Ekström & Westlund, 2019b). However, platform companies have deliberatively communicated that they are not publishers themselves, and thus do not produce content or take responsibility for content like news publishers with editor-in-chiefs do, even though there has been some movement in this direction, as was illustrated by the answer that Facebook CEO Mark Zuckerberg gave to the Cambridge Analytica hearing question regarding what kind of company Facebook is (see chapter 1). Gillespie (2018) traces the emergence of platform companies and formative policy structures that resulted in limited legal requirements in how they curate news content in most markets, and oftentimes only being pressured to moderate content only in cases of terrorism and child pornography.

Platform counterbalancing has to do with the strategically oriented countermeasures publishers engage in to balance their dependence on platform companies. This means taking steps away from an approach oriented towards building a platform presence where they promote and make news content available for free but also stimulate and curate engagement (Chua & Westlund, 2019). Publishers have felt pressured to build a platform presence, but emerging research has also shown that there is growing concern about the long-term developments of "dealing with digital intermediaries" (Kleis Nielsen & Ganter, 2018). There are certainly difficulties and costs involved when attempting to convert attention and engagement associated with consumption on platforms into reader revenues (Cornia, Sehl, Levy, & Nielsen, 2018). Whether people pay attention to news content that they stumble upon or follow on a platform can have some significance when it comes to creating advertising revenues. However, news consumption and audience engagement on platforms non-proprietary to the news media do not necessarily mean people will pay for online news.

As we enter the 2020s, more news publishers have publicly stated that they find their relationship with platform companies problematic, and that they will renegotiate and reposition themselves in the years ahead. Industry representatives report that prominent news organisations such as Schibsted in Norway and Sweden and *The Washington Post* in the US have adopted such approaches (Lindskow, 2020; Seale, 2020). In this context, it is worth noting that the International News Media Association (INMA) has launched the Digital Platform Initiative, which strives towards helping publishers deal with platforms, reducing threats to their financial sustainability. In a 2019 INMA report titled *How to Decode the Publisher-Platform Relationship*, one can learn about the increasingly critical sentiments towards platforms from surveys with news publishers (Whitehead, 2019).

To date, relatively few articles in *Digital Journalism* have approached the interrelationship between publishers and platforms in a critical way. Platform companies and their owners have enormous power in relation to social life and news publishers. Amazon CEO Jeff Bezos, one of the richest men in the world, purchased *The Washington Post*, and Facebook cofounder Chris Hughes acquired the magazine *The New Republic*. A study focusing on the metajournalistic discourse related to Hughes suggests that such a digitally savvy owner will be able to save the magazine and its journalism (Rooney & Creech, 2019). Among other articles we find a study of German public service broadcasters that discusses how Facebook has become a so-called uneasy bedfellow, which news publishers serve with news materials in order to reach out to audiences otherwise difficult to reach (Steiner, Magin, & Stark, 2019). Moreover, Facebook has been widely criticised for how it uses algorithms and humans in curating news content. The company has responded by discussing practices they see as appropriate (Carlson, 2018b). Such criticisms extend to the role Facebook has played, actively and passively, in enabling the spread of disinformation, most notably in conjunction with the 2016 American presidential election (Bakir & McStay, 2018).

A method-oriented article focusing on the multiple meaning of news links concludes that a major issue to consider is that news publishers have outsourced link-sharing to social media platforms like Twitter and Facebook (Ryfe, Mensing, & Kelley, 2016). There are obviously limitations when it comes to the influence journalists and editors exert over how their news content is exposed on Facebook. Using material culture analysis of Facebook's patents, press releases, and data from US Securities and Exchange Commission, DeVito (2017) found nine values built into how the Facebook News Feed operated at the time of the study: friend relationships, explicitly expressed user interests, prior user engagement, implicitly expressed user preferences, post age, platform priorities, page relationships, negatively expressed preferences, and content quality.

The previous section discussed a number of articles focusing on the intersection of journalism and social media, how citizens may stumble upon news in social media, and how they engage with the news via commenting, sharing, etc. In this line of research, it is common to see concerns raised about citizens not accessing news enough to be informed citizens, nor being willing to pay for news, but relatively few scholars have explicitly and critically discussed the many problems arising with platforms from the perspective of publishers. One notable exception is a conceptual article by Myllylahti (2019), in which she elaborates on attention as a key concept. Myllylahti draws on research on attention and platformisation, including some of her own earlier work into platforms and reader revenue (Myllylahti, 2017, 2018). She forwards an analytical framework involving three dimensions: 1) attention as a scarce and fluid commodity, 2) attention as a unit for measurement, and 3) attention as a source of monetisation. Gaining and maintaining audience attention is a key challenge for news publishers, but attention is a fluid commodity, and publishers must successfully measure and monetise on it, while they are under fierce competition with platform companies. In her article, Myllylahti (2019) also discusses general developments of news consumption on and off platforms in 37 countries and how Apple News is surfacing as increasingly important. With this in mind, let us now focus on different digital devices.

4.2 Digital journalism and digital devices

During the first decade of the 21st century there were a considerable number of studies exploring the convergence between print and online news, with which scholars typically studied news sites for desktop. By the time *Digital Journalism* launched in 2013 the field had reached a certain degree of saturation in terms of research into such objects of study. Scholars at the time often developed and discussed distinctions between print media and online news via desktop. Numerous articles focusing on emerging initiatives for "online news sites" have been published, such as a study into live blogs in the UK (Thurman & Walters, 2013), and a comparison of how a dozen news sites cover Israel and Palestine (Segev & Blondheim, 2013), to mention but a few. However, few researchers have cared to differentiate between distinct devices such as desktop or laptop computers, smartphones, tablets, or smart watches. Notable exceptions include a study on how the internet and mobile communication affected print journalism in Zimbabwe) and how mobile and social media were appropriated within a community newspaper in Mozambique (Mare, 2014). This extends to how publishers have approached mobile as part of their cross-media news work (Rodríguez, García, Westlund, & Ulloa-Erazo, 2016; Westlund, 2011, 2014), how they develop communities of practice in relation to sport journalism (Hutchins & Boyle, 2017), and also studies into so-called mobile journalists, also referred to as MoJos (Blankenship, 2016; Kumar & Mohamed Haneef, 2018; Martyn, 2009; Westlund & Quinn, 2018).

There is also longitudinal and multi-method research into varied aspects of news consumption, showing that people engage in monitoring, checking, snacking, scanning, watching, viewing, reading, listening, searching, and clicking (Costera Meijer & Groot Kormelink, 2015), as well as using mobile devices for black witnessing and storytelling via social media such as Twitter (Richardson, 2017). Notwithstanding this, scholars have critically discussed that researchers to a large extent have overlooked research into mobile news (Westlund & Quinn, 2018). Does mobile matter when it comes to how journalists engage in online sourcing, their branding on social media, how algorithms and personalisation work, participation and comment fields, willingness to pay, and so forth? We argue it most certainly does matter, not least because mobile in many markets is the main gateway for accessing the news.

The affordances, designs, and approaches of different devices, and the associated sites and applications used, can differ a great deal. Especially in cases where executives and managers have subscribed to the conception that news publishers "must" customise their approach and content for every device and channel they use. Unsurprisingly, the news accessing patterns for different devices vary, which fortunately is an area that has attracted more significant amounts of research. It is worth noting that there is a long tradition of studies differentiating between newspapers and radioand television organisations (e.g., Elvestad, Phillips, &

Feuerstein, 2018). Similarly, an early cross-cultural study focused on news consumption across broadcast, print, and online, where the latter referred to news sites, and compared this with social media (Nielsen & Schrøder, 2014). Also other scholars at this time gave emphasis to news websites (Zeller, O'Kane, Godo, & Goodrum, 2014).

Research into mobile news has mostly focused on smartphones, but with exceptions including three case studies of digital longforms tailored for tablet devices (Dowling & Vogan, 2015). In the inaugural issue of *Digital Journalism* a review article into mobile news found few studies of tablets and smartphones (Westlund, 2013). In the following years there are a handful of studies into smartphones, journalism, and news, adopting an audience approach to study for example how different platforms and devices are being used as repertoires (Wolf & Schnauber, 2015), and what role mobile news consumption plays (Molyneux, 2018). There are also studies into how mobile devices are used for mobile chat applications such as WhatsApp (Dodds, 2019), into mobility, place-based knowledge, and so-called spatial journalism (Schmitz Weiss, 2015), as well as smartphones for citizen photojournalism and witnessing (Allan & Peters, 2015; Aubert & Nicey, 2015).

Turning towards the most recent developments in the field, we find a 2020 special issue titled "News: Mobilities and Mobiles" (Duffy, Ling, Kim, Tandoc, & Westlund, 2020). It features articles looking into the challenging processes of innovation adoption in the salient case of the mobile social media application WhatsApp (Boczek & Koppers, 2020), the role of mobile news during extraordinary events such as floods (Paul & Sosale, 2020), but also the role of mobile news in everyday life, in relation to mobility (Nelson, 2020) in both intentional and incidental ways (Mäkelä, Boedeker, & Helander, 2020; Stroud, Peacock, & Curry, 2020; Van Damme, Martens, Van Leuven, Vanden Abeele, & De Marez, 2020). Clearly mobile news consumption has gained massive significance, although an empirical national study finds that it has not resulted in increases in political mobilisation (Ohme, 2020). There is also a link between mobile technologies and mobile news with journalism education (Bui & Moran, 2020). We conclude that much literature in digital journalism studies has focused on "online journalism", "news sites", or "social media" without further specification, even when focusing on social media platforms like Twitter, Facebook, and WhatsApp that are mainly used with mobile devices.

4.3 Discussions and conclusions

Our assessment shows that most studies focus on how publishers have built a presence for social media platforms, with many empirical studies based on Twitter data, but also with a growing body of studies advancing our knowledge on platforms such as Facebook, Instagram, WhatsApp, YouTube, and Google. The scholarship published in *Digital Journalism* in the 2010s has not dealt much with social media platforms having significance outside of Europe and North America, such as WeChat and Telegram. Relatively few studies have assessed the publisher–platform relationship in a critical way, but as the journalism sector shifts in this way such scholarship may grow.

Moreover, scholars have repeatedly developed research into online journalism without differentiating between different devices, typically focusing only on practices, behaviours, and attitudes related to desktop. There are most likely several explanations, including but not limited to scholars being familiar with desktop, having largely overlooked the transition to mobile devices in developing their research designs, and better accessibility to desktop related data compared to mobile. There is some research into mobile news consumption, but less into how journalists and publishers deal with considerations of mobile technology in their practice.

In light of the 4 A's (S. C. Lewis & Westlund, 2015a), we find that relatively few studies have focused on the technologies and platforms per se, and the agency inscribed into the technological actant (exceptions include Diakopoulos, 2015; Helberger, 2019). Scholars have typically studied either how social actors approach emerging technologies, such as journalists appropriating Twitter or analytics in their daily practice, or they have studied how audiences are dealing with the changing mediascape in terms of accessing and engaging with news via social media platforms. It is obviously challenging and time-consuming to adopt holistic approaches to the study of actors, actants, and audiences. However, the stream of studies focusing on only one of the A's results in more fragmented knowledge. Moreover, problems arise in terms of comparing different studies. Even if we constrain ourselves to comparing findings about journalism and platforms in the salient case of Twitter, we will find it difficult to synthesise findings from surveys with journalists from country X and year X, with studies of how they interact on Twitter in country Y and year Y, and interviews with audiences in country Z from year Z about their attitudes to journalists tweeting. Ultimately, scholars should develop more holistic and critical approaches to the study of how publishers approach platforms and digital devices, and the consequences for how citizens access and engage with the news.

5 The theories

How digital journalism is understood[1]

Let's say a news company you know of wants to innovate. This news company, which we will call *The Daily Times*, has suffered massive declines in both readership and ad revenues since the turn of the millennium, but now it has entered into a partnership with a tech start-up to create a new journalistic product to be distributed on Snapchat. You are curious about this development and want to initiate a research project to investigate it. But how do you frame it theoretically? If your background is in sociology, you might want to research how the developments at *The Daily Times* affect journalism's position and role in society, if and how they change what it means to be a journalist, or other aspects related to journalism as a profession, a social institution, field, or system. If you are more interested in political science, you perhaps would like to research to what degree the case changes journalism's democratic function, if it manages to get new audiences interested in public affairs, or other aspects related to journalism's position in the public sphere. If your interests align with Science and Technology Studies (STS), you are maybe interested in analysing how technology and humans interact and who and what shapes the innovation process and outcome.

If you have a background in language studies, you might want to investigate how journalistic genres develop in the new Snapchat product, if new rhetorical strategies can be detected, how the new journalism creates meaning through linguistic, discursive, or semiotic features, or other aspects related to the production, distribution, or consumption of multimodal texts. If you are more interested in analysing the case from a cultural studies perspective, you perhaps want to figure out how the Snapchat product affects how audiences relate to news in their everyday lives, or if and how the case changes the journalists' self-perception and feelings of identity, or maybe what kinds of narratives the new initiative creates. If you are interested in philosophy, you might want to research if and how the journalists, when working with the new Snapchat product, create knowledge and make judgments about what is true and not. If you are a historian, you might search in the history of media and technology to find similarities with the recent development. If you are an economist or business and administration scholar, you might be interested in how the new product alters the supply and demand of and for journalism and news, or how reward systems affect the decision making of the actors involved in the innovation process, or how organisational mechanisms in the news company and the tech start-up affect the process.

In other words: The possibilities are almost endless. Digital journalism studies is both a cross-disciplinary field, meaning that the same case can be researched from a variety of different disciplines, and it is interdisciplinary, meaning that multiple disciplinary perspectives can be combined in one research project about the case. This cross- and interdisciplinary nature of digital journalism studies means that there are a substantial number of theories that potentially can be used to explore and frame a research project on *The Daily Times* case. Those that you eventually deploy reflect where your research interests lie and, evidently, which research question(s) you would like to find answers to.

Throughout this chapter we will use this imagined research project to look at the many ways in which theory matters for research in general and digital journalism studies in particular. We will look at how theories from a variety of disciplines can be utilised and/or developed to answer a myriad of possible research questions related to this one case. In chapters 3 and 4, we discussed the topics and objects that preoccupy digital journalism studies. We showed how the field has been dominated by an emphasis on technologies and platforms, and also to an increasing degree on audiences. This does not mean that everything about digital journalism studies concerns technologies, platforms, and audiences, nor does it mean that the theoretical perspectives, frameworks, and assumptions researchers interested in digital journalism make use of and develop are about technologies, platforms, and audiences. Digital journalism studies is much more. It is a research field for scholars in all kinds of disciplines – and therefore it can be understood and theorised in many different ways.

In this chapter we will take a closer look at this role of theory in the field, what theories are commonly used and how they contribute to making sense of digital journalism. We will also identify some theoretical shortcomings of digital journalism studies, but first we need to discuss the possible ways in which theory can be understood and what *attitudes* towards theory are possible to for such a research project like *The Daily Times* case.

5.1 What is theory and why does it matter?

When you design your research project on the *The Daily Times* case one of the first things you need to think about is what kind of attitude towards theory you have. To what degree do you base your research on theoretical assumptions? Do you want to test a specific theory, or do you want to develop theory? Whatever you choose, you will relate to theory in one way or the other.

The word "theory" has many connotations. It can mean the opposite of practice. Theory can also be explanatory or mean something that can be tested, verified, or falsified. Theory can be grand or grounded, inductive, deductive, or abductive. It can be rational, critical, pragmatic, or normative. Theory usually means one thing to a natural scientist and something very different to a researcher from the humanities. Social sciences, in turn, can encompass the whole spectrum. Mjøset (2006) distinguishes between three different attitudes towards theory in the social sciences:

1 The *standard attitude*, which implies an understanding of theory as accumulated knowledge based on regularities as law-like or idealised as possible. This attitude involves, in its purest sense, derivation of hypotheses from macro-theories and testing them on empirical material.
2 The *social-philosophical attitude*, which implies an understanding of theory as something that is a result of investigations into how the human mind organises knowledge. This attitude typically involves generating theoretical concepts suited to frame and interpret aspects of modernity.
3 The *pragmatist-participatory attitude*, which implies an understanding of theory as knowledge of observable patterns accumulated in "local research frontiers" consisting of previously conducted empirical inquires of similar cases and previously developed grounded theories related to the same topic.

Given the cross- and interdisciplinary nature of digital journalism studies, we can expect to find all three attitudes towards theory in inquiries within the research field. As such, all three attitudes could be applied to a research project about the *The Daily Times* case. For instance, you could apply Bourdieu's field theory and investigate to what degree this partnership between the legacy news company and a tech start-up affects journalism as a social field. If you formulate hypotheses based on field theory and test those hypotheses on the empirical findings of your case study, you apply the standard attitude towards theory. Or you could treat the case as an example to illustrate aspects of network theory, for instance related to what happens to a network when new "nodes" (the tech start-up, Snapchat) are introduced to an existing network (the news network). Then you apply the social-philosophical attitude. Or you could sample both theoretical and empirical knowledge from previous research on similar cases and aim at advancing that knowledge through an analysis of your case. Then you apply the pragmatist-participatory attitude. However, choosing the attitude towards theory is only the first step towards a research design. The second step would be to figure out exactly what theoretical perspective would be relevant and, consequently, which research questions to formulate.

5.2 The multitude of theories in digital journalism studies

In chapter 1 we argued that sociological perspectives are most common in digital journalism studies, followed by technological and political science perspectives (see Figure 1.1 in section 1.3.1). However, what is striking about digital journalism studies is that both sociological and political science perspectives are quite often combined with an emphasis on technology, implying either that technological aspects are what is being studied or that researchers apply social or political science theory that is sensitive to the role of technology. Thirty-eight percent of the 172 abstracts we analysed in *Digital Journalism* are marked by such technology-oriented sociological or political sciences perspectives. A typical examples is Usher (2013) who employs news norms theory and the theory of social construction of technology to analyse how *Al Jazeera*'s English website used web metrics for tracking and understanding audience behaviour.

Another typical feature of the research published in *Digital Journalism* is that a majority of it adopts a pragmatist-participatory attitude towards theory and develops middle-range or even micro-theory from empirical data. In this respect, digital journalism studies is no different from journalism studies or even communication studies in general (Ahva & Steensen, 2020; Bryant & Miron, 2004; Kamhawi & Weaver, 2003). The pragmatist-participatory attitude towards theory means that the research does not start with assumptions or perspectives derived from grand theories, but rather builds on previously established empirical knowledge in an inductive, grounded theory-like fashion in order to advance knowledge. Half of the 172 abstracts we analysed derive from such an attitude towards theory. A typical example is Johnston (2016) who analyses the uses of social media and user-generated content by journalists in the

BBC World News newsroom and the effects this has on the role of the journalists.

In the other half of the 172 abstracts from *Digital Journalism* we find 69 different theories and conceptual constructs. Only 11 of those are mentioned in more than two abstracts, implying that digital journalism studies is much about finding new ways to conceptualise the research. A good number of the articles published in the journal are conceptual pieces that discuss theory or introduce new conceptualisations or theoretical frameworks. Some of the most influential articles published in the journal (in terms of citation metrics) fall into this category, like Lewis and Westlund (2015a) who argue for developing a socio-technical emphasis for the study of institutional news production.

In the following sub-sections we take a closer look at some of the most influential and common theories used to frame and interpret empirical findings within digital journalism studies, not only in articles published in the journal *Digital Journalism*, but in a broader sense.

5.2.1 Digital journalism as a social system

Sociological perspectives imply that digital journalism is understood as a kind of *social system in which certain roles are performed and practices undertaken*. A range of social system-related macro-theories have been used to explain and explore the role that digital journalism plays in societies, why it matters, what makes it different from other forms of communication and other parts of society, and how it changes. To return to our case study of *The Daily Times*, the tech start-up, and Snapchat: If your primary research interest in investigating this case is to explore how it relates to or affects journalism as a social system, you have a range of theoretical options. Luhmann's **theory of social systems** can help to explain digital journalism's position in a society by how it differentiates itself from other social systems (like for instance the social system the tech start-up initially belongs to) and creates boundaries of meaning (Loosen, 2015). Bourdieu's **field theory** has been used to analyse the connections between journalistic organisations, practices, products, and professionals, on the one side, and other social fields, like for instance advertising (Q. Wang, 2018) on the other, or how digital interlopers (like for instance tech-workers at the tech start-up) challenge the boundaries of the journalistic field (Eldridge II, 2017). Like field theory, **new institutionalism** is a social system theory that mediates "the impact of macro-level forces on micro-level actions" (Ryfe, 2006, p. 137). Analysing digital journalism as an institution means analysing the presuppositions and tacit knowledge that guide journalistic practice across digital newsrooms, news organisations, and other journalistic organisations. Related to our case, new institutionalism could be applied to analyse how the tacit knowledge of both the journalists at *The Daily Times* and the technologists and entrepreneurs at the tech start-up affect their ability to cooperate.

Central to these theories is that they provide explanations and questions from a macro perspective for how an institution/field/system like journalism functions and develops in digital societies through analysis of how individual behaviour coincides with larger, cross-organisational structures. As such, social system theories provide frameworks for analysing interplays between mental structures (norms, values, ideals), material structures (economy, technology), and agency in digital journalism. We find ways of analysing the same interplay also in middle-range theories like organisational theory and hierarchy of influences theory. The difference is that such theories do not aim at explaining societies on a macro level. **Organisational theory** provides a framework for understanding how various kinds of organisations (like the news company and the tech start-up) are configured and reconfigured by internal and external structures, and by the actions of different kinds of professions and labour that are part of the organisation. Organisational theory has been applied in digital journalism studies to analyse, for example, how specific beats, like science journalism (Lublinski, 2011), develop in a digitised news environment. News production studies also take news organisations as their starting point and analyse how agency and mental and material structures shape how news is produced in digitised news rooms (Domingo & Paterson, 2011; Usher, 2014). Such studies have been important in advancing our knowledge of how classical middle-range theories of journalism, like theories of **news values** (see for instance Harcup & O'Neill, 2017) and **gatekeeping theory** (see for instance Bro & Wallberg, 2015) hold up in a digital age. Such theories could also be relevant to the *The Daily Times* case, if the primary aim is to understand how specific beats, genres, or types of journalism develop with the partnership between the news company and the tech start-up in place; or how the partnership and Snapchat as a publication and distribution platform affect what is considered news (news values) or who gets to decide what is newsworthy (gatekeeping).

Recognising that journalism in digital times has become increasingly independent of news organisations and influenced by all kinds of structures and agency on macro-, meso-, and micro-levels, the **hierarchy of influence theory** introduced by Shoemaker and Reese (1996) provides a model of the levels that influence digital journalism: from the macro-social systems, via social institutions and organisations, to the micro-levels of routine practices and individuals. Similarly, **practice theory**

(Bourdieu, 1977; Schatzki, 2001) has been used to analyse how activities, materiality, and discursive reflexivity connected to journalism shape what digital journalism is and why it develops as it does, preferably without preconceived ideas on who the key agents are, what they produce and within what kind of organisational framework journalism operates (Ahva, 2017). Both these theories have obvious relevance to our case, if you want to investigate how the partnership and Snapchat influence journalism as practice.

The theory of **media logic** (Altheide & Snow, 1979) could be equally relevant, especially if the concern is to investigate how the organisational, technological, and aesthetic dimensions of the companies, platforms, and products involved work together in supporting the creation of content and how that content is shared. Even though the theory was developed in an age of mass media, it has proved valuable in analysis of how different media and platforms in digital times differ in their logics and how "polymedia channels" become more and more contextualised in everyday lives (Thimm, Anastasiadis, & Einspänner-Pflock, 2018).

In our analysis of abstracts of articles published in *Digital Journalism* between 2013 and 2019 (N = 172) we find that many of the above-mentioned theories are among the most used. Gatekeeping theory, field theory, institutional theory, and hierarchy of influence theory are among the 11 theories we found explicitly mentioned on two occasions or more in the abstracts analysed. Sociological theories related to **professionalism**, which are the most common theories in journalism studies as a whole (Ahva & Steensen, 2020), are also common in digital journalism studies, but to a lesser extent and with decreasing popularity in the journal *Digital Journalism*, when we look at how keywords belonging to the thematic cluster *professionalism* have developed. The keywords belonging to this cluster – like *values, norms, role, professional identity, autonomy, ideals, skills, standards*, and others – were used in 3 percent of the articles published between 2013 and 2015, but only in 1 percent of articles published between 2017 and 2019. However, major research projects like the Worlds of Journalism study (see Hanitzsch, Hanusch, Ramaprasad, & De Beer, 2019) have been preoccupied with how notions of journalistic professionalism develop in a digital age in various cultural contexts, so it would be unfair to claim that digital journalism studies is not interested in how journalism develops as a profession in digital times. And professionalism would be an obvious framework for the *The Daily Times* case, if the main research concern prompting analysis is to understand how the partnership with both the tech start-up and Snapchat affect the role of journalists at *The Daily Times*, the norms and values they adhere to, and so forth. That said, one reason for the decreased popularity of professionalism as a theoretical framework in *Digital Journalism* might be that this framework has been criticised for limiting the domain that is seen as a valid information source about journalism and hence potentially omitting the role of participating non-journalists in the construction of journalism (Ahva, 2017).

5.2.2 Digital journalism as a socio-technical practice

A recurring theme in digital journalism studies is the connection between technology, power, and change. Is technology a powerful driving force behind all the changes that mark what digital journalism is becoming, or is technology merely one of several things that influence how journalism develops? Or is it perhaps the other way around: that the developments in digital journalism are the things that shape technological developments?

Influences from -STS- have enriched digital journalism studies with a nuanced and theoretically informed understanding of the relationship between technology and journalism. **Technological determinism**, which presupposes that technologies are blind to social and cultural diversity and enforce change wherever they are introduced, used to dominate research on digital journalism (Steensen, 2011b). But the works of scholars like Bijker (1995), Bolter and Grusin (Bolter, 2001; Bolter & Grusin, 1999), Manovich (2001), Mosco (2004), and perhaps most importantly Latour (2005) have shown that technology is not a blind determinant of change. Technology is socially and culturally shaped. Theories like **the social construction (or shaping) of technology (SCOT)** (Bijker, Hughes, & Pinch, 1987) have been adapted to the analysis of journalism in digital times, most notably by Boczkowski in his book *Digitizing the News* (2004), which paved the way for understanding the interplay between technology, materiality, and social practice related to the production of digital journalism.

Another relevant theory, which has been much used in digital journalism studies and which represents a middle ground between technological determinisms and SCOT, is **affordance theory**, which originally was an ecological theory related to human perceptions of what the environment can offer (Gibson, 1979). Applied to technology, affordance theory emphasises how the possibilities (and restraints) of certain technologies can be utilised in their context of use (Conole & Dyke, 2004). One important aspect to technological affordance theory is that the affordances are not understood as objective characteristics of the technology in question, but rather as something that is *perceived* to have certain affordances in given contexts, what Nagy and Neff (2015) call "imagined affordances". Related to our research case, affordance theory can be used to analyse how the imagined/perceived affordances of Snapchat create both possibilities and restraints for practicing journalism on the platform. A technological determinist approach to the same question would imply that Snapchat is seen as determining the journalistic practice, regardless of the social and culture context of the practice, while a SCOT approach would imply an assumption that Snapchat is a flexible technology that is shaped by the social context of its application.

Both SCOT and affordance theory acknowledge that technology enters into a relationship with social contexts and that human actors have an effect on what kind of impact technologies have. They also have in common that technology usually is the starting point of an inquiry and that the relevant social context is easily identifiable. However, the increasing uncertainty as to *where* journalism is to be found, *who* produces it, on *what* technological platforms it exists, and *how* various groups of professionals and amateurs participate and cooperate in its coming into existence in digital times has led to the popularity of socio-technical theories that do not take anything for granted, like **actor-network theory (ANT)** (Latour, 2005). ANT is a middle-range social systems theory with no preconceived ideas about who and what shape a social system. It emphasises not only the mutual shaping of journalism and technology but also juxtaposes human, technological, and material actors (or actants, which is the most common word for human and non-human actors in ANT) as equally important to this mutual shaping. The theory has been praised for its non-deterministic, unbiased, and empirical orientation (see Primo & Zago, 2015 for a discussion), its adaptability to digital journalism in particular (Domingo et al., 2015), but also critiqued for being a methodological approach and not a theory, and for its inclination to produce nothing more than dull descriptions (Benson, 2017).

Similar to ANT, other network theories like **homophily**, **resource dependence**, and **social influence theory** (see Fu, 2016 for an overview) open up the empirical field to include potential actors, which the researcher did not think of beforehand, while simultaneously emphasising the relations between them and the actions and work being done through those relations. The use of the keyword "network" has in recent years grown significantly in digital journalism studies, as have spatial keywords related to "ecosystems" and "landscapes". Reese (2016, p. 10) refers to "the ecosystem shift" in theories of journalism and connects this to the emergence of digital platforms that have made some of the classical conceptual categorisations invalid.

Returning to the *The Daily Times* case, an ANT approach could be appropriate if the main aim of the research is to understand, in descriptive manners, who and what are important for how the new journalistic product on Snapchat turns out. If you are more interested in the relations and power dynamics between the organisations involved (*The Daily Times*, the tech start-up, Snapchat, and potentially other organisations with relations to the news company or the tech start-up), you might want to analyse the case for instance as an affinity network (Fu, 2016). Or, if you feel (actor-)network theory is too unstructured to apply, you can choose a more structured adaptation, like Lewis and Westlund's (2015a) 4As framework, which provides a model for analysing the actors, actants, audiences, and activities involved in producing the new Snapchat output.

5.2.3 Digital journalism as a democratic force

If your research interests lie not so much with the social or socio-technical, but rather with journalism's link to political systems and the public sphere, you probably want to apply a political science perspective on the case. Political science is the third most common disciplinary framework in digital journalism studies, according to our journal analysis, and it usually means that digital journalism *is seen as a democratic force that shapes public discourse.*

A number of potential research questions which would require a political science perspective can be addressed to explore the *The Daily Times* case: What does the new Snapchat channel contribute to the public sphere? Does it enhance awareness about public affairs, or is it mainly a provider of entertainment? Does it allow new voices to be heard? Does it reach new audiences and contribute to their interest in public affairs? Does it address the audience as (passive) consumers, (active) citizens, or in another way? To what degree does it allow audiences to participate? And how does the tech start-up and the whole Snapchat affair influence the news company's self-perceived societal role as for instance a watchdog, populist mobiliser, interpreter, disseminator, fourth estate, custodian of conscience, or other professional role conceptions (Glasser & Ettema, 1989; Hanitzsch, 2017; Mellado, 2019)?

Many of these questions would require some kind of democracy or public sphere theory. There are long, historic ties between journalism and democracy/public sphere theories. A free, independent press that facilitates a public sphere in which ideas and politics can be disseminated, debated, critiqued, and shaped has been considered a cornerstone for democracy ever since the Age of Enlightenment, in which catchphrases like Thomas Jefferson's "information is the currency of democracy" began to dominate the democracy discourse (Zelizer, 2013, p. 463). Theories of journalism and democracy are usually normative theories, implying that they prescribe what role journalism *should* have in a society and what a democracy *should* be like. Embedded in such normative theories is the notion that journalism is a prerequisite for democracy and vice versa; journalism and democracy are so intertwined that the one cannot exist without the other.

Such normative theories of journalism (and democracy) have been criticised for a number of reasons. First, they cannot explain how and why journalism exists in semi- or non-democratic societies. Siebert, Peterson, and Schram (1963) addressed this problem in their categorisation of how journalism functions in various political systems expressed as **the four theories of the press**: the authoritarian, libertarian, social responsibility, and Soviet-totalitarian. However, the four theories of the press did not provide an escape from normative theory, as it was discursively embedded within a libertarian logic that clearly ranked the four categories along an axis from good to bad (Nerone, 1995). Several revisions of the four theories of the press and alternative models have since been suggested, all of which are based on some degrees of normativity (see Christians, Glasser, McQuail, Nordenstreng, & White, 2009, chapter 1 for a review). Moreover, normative theories linking journalism and democracy tend to disregard the fact that journalism, especially in our digital age, is not the only channel through which trustworthy information can flow in a society and a public sphere marked by a diversity of opinions can be established. Blogs, social media, citizen journalism, and other information channels have democratised public speech, and Zelizer (2013) has therefore, and for other reasons, suggested it is time to put democracy theory to rest in journalism studies.

Nevertheless, democracy theories enable us to understand the role that digital journalism plays as a facilitator of the public sphere and how it covers issues that require public attention. The so-called **procedural or competitive democracy theories** have long framed journalism studies and guided researchers' attention towards the role that journalism plays in providing information to citizens as voters between the elections and the ways in which politicians compete over power in the public sphere, while **participatory and deliberative democracy theories** became more prominent in the 1990s as journalism moved to digitised spaces (Strömbäck, 2005). These models invite us to examine and assess whether journalism enables or restricts civic agency and reasoning beyond the moment of voting, and the role of public discourse in the formation of the political culture (e.g., Ettema, 2007). As a more middle-range theory developed within communication studies, **agenda–setting theory** (McCombs & Shaw, 1972) provides a framework for analysing how journalism shapes the public sphere and consequently the ways in which we, as the public, understand the world. Theories of **second-level agenda setting** (Ghanem,

1997) and **inter-media agenda setting** (Danielian & Reese, 1989) refine agenda-setting theory in ways that make it more relevant for digital journalism studies. They provide frameworks for analysing how the media discuss issues that have already made the agenda and how certain media (like elite newspapers) influence what other media (like social media) have on their agenda. Returning to the *The Daily Times* case for a moment, one question based on an inter-media agenda-setting framework, could be to analyse how the Snapchat initiative affects the agenda on Snapchat in general.

5.2.4 Digital journalism as post-industrial business endeavour

The financial crises in general and the economic distress of journalism in digital times in particular have caused an increased interest in digital journalism as business, its organisational structures, and its economic sustainability. Economic theories like **rational choice theory**, which has been used to analyse journalists as "rational actors seeking to maximize materialistic and non-materialistic rewards" (Fengler & Ruß-Mohl, 2008, p. 667); **path dependency theory**, which can explain why legacy news organisations have difficulties coping with change (Koch, 2008); and more audience-centric economic theories like **uses and gratification theory**, which can be used to analyse emerging patterns of news consumption (Diddi & LaRose, 2006), have been applied.

The same holds for **organisational development theory**, which has been used, among other things, to assess the perceptions and attitudes that top newsroom managers and journalists have about initiatives aimed at changing newsroom cultures (Gade, 2004). As such, organisational development theory has some similarities with innovation theories, especially **diffusion of innovation theory** (E. M. Rogers, 2003), which has been used in digital journalism studies to assess how processes of innovation and thereby change proceed in an organisation like a news company.

Interestingly, there is a tendency within digital journalism studies that keywords such as "media industry" and "economic theory" are decreasing in popularity and being replaced by a variety of more flexible, individual-focused, and business-related conceptualisations, such as "sustainability" or "entrepreneurialism" (Ahva & Steensen, 2020, p. 48). This shift is connected to a situation where the journalism industry as a clearly demarcated branch within the media industry needs to be rethought – as proposed by the notion of "post-industrial journalism" (C. W. Anderson, Bell, & Shirky, 2015) and Deuze and Witschge's (2020) work on "Beyond Journalism", in which the authors stress the need to theorise journalism beyond legacy institutions and organisations and include the increasingly entrepreneurial nature of journalism. This rethinking of journalism as industry and business thereby represents a move from organisational enterprises to individual entrepreneurship, a move that emphasises how individual journalists can (and should) reinvent themselves as independent entrepreneurs by starting a company outside of legacy news organisations. Hence concepts and theories from management and business studies, such as **business model canvas** (Singer, 2016), are applied to address how journalists can see change and disruption as business opportunities (Briggs, 2012).

The *Daily Times* case, in which a tech start-up becomes involved in journalism, can certainly be analysed with such a business model canvas perspectives in mind. Economic theories could also easily be applied to the case, if the primary interest is to understand why the organisations involved, the journalists, the tech start-up workers, and the audiences choose to act as they do. Organisational development theory could also be relevant if the aim is to investigate how the news company facilitated and reacted to the change brought forth by the partnership with the tech start-up. And, obviously, innovation theory is relevant if it is the process of innovation itself, and how such processes unfold, that is of interest.

5.2.5 Digital journalism as cultural production and discourse

Perspectives from cultural and language studies occupy a smaller part (about 9 percent combined, see Figure 1.1 in chapter 1) of digital journalism studies, as revealed in our analysis of article abstracts, than in journalism studies in general (Ahva & Steensen, 2020; Steensen & Ahva, 2015). Traditionally, analysing journalism through the lenses of cultural theory has implied questioning what is presupposed in journalism, unravelling how journalists view themselves, trying to understand the diversity of journalism, and connecting journalistic practices and products to questions of power, ideology, class, ethnicity, gender, identity, and so on. However, it seems as if the cultural analysis of digital journalism is more interested in how journalism intersects with everyday life, with the "moment at which media production becomes communication and culture – the moment of the use in the circumstances of everyday life" (Hartley, 2008, p. 47). This reflects what Costera Meijer (2020) has labelled "the audience turn" in journalism studies, a turn which is quite visible in our analysis of articles in *Digital Journalism*, since "audience" is the second biggest thematic cluster of keywords next to "platform" (see chapter 2, section 2.3). The audience cluster comprises keywords that typically signal political science perspectives (like "citizen", "participation", and "public"), but also several that signal more cultural dimensions, like "readership", "amateur", "perception", "community", and "reader contract").

There are many potential research questions related to our *Daily Times* case which would require a theoretical framework from cultural or language studies. Some examples could be: How does the partnership affect journalists' self-perception and identity? To what degree does the Snapchat product alter the function of journalism as a meaning-making system? What genre conventions are utilised on Snapchat and how does this affect the journalist-text-audience relationship? How does the new product affect journalism as a discursive practice? And how do the news company's ambitions with the Snapchat product align with how it is perceived by audiences?

Critical theory has traditionally been strongly connected with the cultural analysis of journalism, especially as related to neo-Marxism and the Frankfurt school of thought. This implies an ambition to unmask the social and ideological power structures embedded in journalism and to uncover the discrepancies between journalistic self-perception and "metajournalistic discourse" (Carlson, 2016) on the one hand, and the actual expressions and meaning production systems of journalism on the other. Hence, language-based traditions of studying journalism are closely related to cultural ones. The field of **semiotics**, in which text is understood as not only written language, but also as still and moving images, body language, and so on, has been important in recognising journalism as visual culture and the diversity through which journalism produces meaning. Language studies increasingly also emphasises the social and cultural situatedness of digital journalism texts, which requires that the studies of text are informed by material and contextual dimensions, too (Richardson, 2008, p. 2).

Discourse theory (recently discussed and developed, for example, in Kelsey, 2015), **narrative theory** (e.g., J. Johnston & Graham, 2012), and **genre theories** (Smith & Higgins, 2013) can be important to analyse digital journalism as a meaning-making system. Van Dijk (2009, p. 193) has underlined that a major dimension in discourse analytical studies of journalism is the ideological nature of news. The approach can therefore help in examining the expression and reproduction of ideology in digital journalism, the axiomatic beliefs underlying the social representations shared by a group. Significantly, van Dijk points out that the role of discourse in reproducing racism, nationalism, and sexism should be more carefully studied in the future.

5.3 The theoretical blind spots of digital journalism studies

The theories we have discussed represent the main disciplinary perspectives found in digital journalism studies. However, they are not the only theories employed, nor are they the only theories that might be of value. The most significant form of theoretical knowledge found in digital journalism studies is perhaps the increasing body of accumulated knowledge concerning what digital journalism is, where it is to be found, who produces, distributes, and consumes it, and why (or if) it matters. This knowledge is accumulated through empirical investigations and conceptual discussions in grounded theory-inspired research designs and attitudes towards theory. It is a kind of knowledge that is crucial to have and to constantly update when your object of study is constantly changing, as is the case with digital journalism.

There are, however, some potential problems with this kind of knowledge accumulation and theory building and framing. The first problem is related to the emphasis on *change* that dominates the field. We will discuss this problem in more depth in the next chapter, in section 6.2.2, so here we will only point to one potential reason for this emphasis on change and the potential blind spots it creates, namely that there seems to be a lack of historic perspectives in digital journalism studies, at least in articles published in *Digital Journalism*. This becomes evident when we look at the sources referenced in articles published in the journal. The 350 articles published between 2013 and issue 4, 2019, have a total of 14,794 references. Fifty-nine percent of these references point to research published after 2010, and only 13 percent point to research published before 2000. In other words, there is a lack of connection with findings from the past and a preoccupation with the present and the future in digital journalism studies. No doubt, an emphasis on the present is understandable, perhaps even logical, in a field like digital journalism studies, which to a certain degree is determined to investigate the current changes to its object of study due to recent technological developments. However, this does not mean that such inquiries should only emphasise what is changing, and only look at such changes from the perspectives of recent theories and research. We therefore conclude that digital journalism studies should have a stronger connection with the past in order to better understand the present and predict the future.

A second blind spot is that digital journalism studies has a social science bias. There are many reasons why digital journalism scholars should view digital journalism, and other forms of journalism for that matter, predominantly as a social phenomenon. A dominance of social science perspectives and approaches is therefore not in itself a problem. One might even argue that without such prominence, digital journalism studies would neglect the social, political, and to a certain extent cultural ramifications of the digital on journalism. However, approaches from the humanities are also capable of analysing journalism as a social (and cultural) phenomenon. When perspectives from the humanities are marginalised as they seem to have been with the ways in which digital journalism studies has developed in *Digital Journalism* (see Figure 1.1 in chapter 1), and when methodological approaches are increasingly geared towards computation and big data (as we will discuss in chapter 7), crucial elements of digital journalism might be overlooked. As argued by Steensen et al. (2019, p. 336):

> The future reader who consults *Digital Journalism* to find out how ideas and discourses were constructed in journalistic texts in the 2010s, how journalism created meaning of and for the societies and cultures it served, how journalism functioned as a system of knowledge creation, and how such questions were connected to historic developments, is likely to be disappointed. To provide answers to such questions, digital journalism studies should to a greater extent embrace the disciplinary perspectives and qualitative methodologies of the humanities.

Even though digital journalism studies no doubt is highly cross- and interdisciplinary, in spite of these biases, there seems to be an underdeveloped potential of connecting not only with fields within the humanities, but also those fields related to technology, like computer science, informatics, and information science. Boczkowski and Mitchelstein (2017) argue that digital journalism studies is marked by an inability to connect empirical findings across other domains of digital culture, and by a lack of conceptual exchanges with other fields and disciplines. It seems obvious that digital journalism studies should move beyond a topical interest in technology and connect with fields and disciplines like computer science and informatics on a more theoretical level. For instance, the field of theoretical computer science "provides concepts and languages to capture the essence, in algorithmic and descriptive terms, of any system from specification to efficient implementation" (Van Leeuwen, 1990 Preface). As digital journalism becomes increasingly dependent on algorithmic processing (see chapter 7, section 7.2), acquiring such concepts and languages seems crucial for digital journalism scholarship. Similarly, theoretical understandings of information transformation across natural and engineered systems, which is the essence of informatics as an academic field, seem important for digital journalism scholarship. Practices of digital journalism, especially those related to investigative journalism, are increasingly preoccupied with the analysis of massive amounts of unstructured data, which requires both methodological and theoretical knowledge in order to make sense. Here, digital journalism scholarship needs not only the same kind of knowledge to assess such practices of journalism critically, but also the knowledge to experiment with how digital journalism can make sense of such information transformations. Some examples of the latter already exist, either from within informatics itself, like Wiedemann et al.'s (2018) experimental research on developing tools for the analysis of massive amounts of documents like the Panama Papers or similar big leaks, or from interdisciplinary cooperation like Maiden et al.'s (2018), Nyre's (2015, 2012), and Backholm et al.'s (2018) experimentations with new journalistic applications.

Note

1 This chapter is based on and partly reuses and further develops arguments, findings, and phrases previously published by Ahva and Steensen (2020), Steensen and Ahva (2015), and Steensen et al. (2019).

6 The assumptions

The underlying normativity of digital journalism studies

In the previous chapter, we discussed the role of theory in digital journalism studies and the many theoretical perspectives through which a research project investigating aspects of digital journalism can be framed. We used an imagined case as an example: a news company that had partnered with a tech start-up to develop a new journalistic product to be distributed on Snapchat. We showed how this one case can be analysed based on a myriad of research questions reflecting different theoretical perspectives in order to acquire new theoretical or empirical knowledge. Some of these research questions were quite neutral in their quest for new knowledge, while others were based on ideas of what journalism should be, like: does the Snapchat product allow new voices be heard? Does it reach new audiences and contribute to their interest in public affairs? These two questions presuppose that new voices *should* be heard in digital journalism, that digital journalism *should* reach new audiences, and that it *should* make people interested in public affairs. In other words: These research questions are based on normative ideas and theories.

Traditionally, much of journalism studies has been rooted in such normative ideas and theories, especially related to the role of journalism in societies. This includes journalism's ability to treat its audience like informed citizens and raise awareness and public engagement on matters of perceived importance, and, consequently, on what is good and bad journalism (Benson, 2008). Our (normative) position is that there is nothing wrong with normativity in research in general and in digital journalism studies in particular. However, normativity is a problem if it is hidden, unproblematised, and masked as apparent neutrality.

There are at least three ways in which such problematic normativity could occur in digital journalism studies. First, researchers in the field should be aware of how digital journalism as practice challenges certain norms concerning what journalism is and should be. Second, digital journalism researchers should be aware of the norms potentially embedded in the ways in which they ask and frame research questions. Third, the methods researchers choose are not neutral. They carry with them certain ways of viewing the world and specific norms related to what knowledge is and how it can be obtained.

We return to the potential problems of normativity in methodology further in chapter 7. In this chapter we predominantly discuss the normativity related to the formulation and framing of research questions in digital journalism studies, and the ways in which this normativity is quite often hidden and therefore in need of more transparency and researcher awareness. Robinson et al. (2019, p. 374) argue that "normative awareness" should be one of the commitments of digital journalism scholars. Our key argument is that digital journalism scholars need to be more reflexive about their normative presuppositions, implying also a reflexivity towards how the normativity of other scholars might influence their work. It is, for example, quite common to argue that investigating developments in digital journalism are important because journalism is important to the democratic functioning of a society. Such normative assumptions are becoming increasingly problematic, as digital journalism has many other social functions, as new information streams can carry the same function, and as digital journalism exists also in non-democratic societies, among other reasons (for more in-depth discussions of this problem, see Peters, 2019a; Zelizer, 2013).

Kreiss and Brennen (2016) argue there are four norms that are particularly present in digital journalism studies, namely that digital journalism should be: 1) *participatory*, since new technologies and platforms allow for a transformation of audiences from passive consumers to active participants; 2) *deinstitutionalised*, implying that the legacy news institutions should give up power and that processes and products of journalism should be decentralised; 3) *innovative*, to utilise new technology and create new business models better equipped to deal with the digital economy; and 4) *entrepreneurial*, implying that journalists should be self-starters, brand themselves, and build their own funding and audiences. Being aware of such norms and how they affect the research is important to the academic quality of digital journalism.

In this chapter we first look at the ways in which the relationship between digital technology and journalism has been, and still is, normatively framed in two opposite future-predictions in digital journalism studies: either in optimistic terms as a saviour of journalism and potentially also democracy, or as being part of a discourse of crisis in which digital technology ruins everything that is good about journalism. Then we look particularly at the norms embedded in the discourse of innovation that dominates much of digital journalism studies. In the concluding section, we will briefly discuss some ways in which we think it is important that digital journalism studies researchers *do* take a normative position.

6.1 The normative future-predictions of digital journalism studies

On 15 October 2009, the then editor-in-chief of the Norwegian tabloid newspaper *Dagbladet*, Anne Aasheim, stood in front of some of the members of the New Media Network, an independent Norwegian consortium for media companies, politicians, consultants, and researchers interested in new media trends and developments. Aasheim was about to give a speech on how *Dagbladet* was coping with convergence in times of crisis. She started out by saying: "Today I feel like being an optimist".[1]

She paused and looked as if she were expecting some kind of reaction reflecting disbelief among members of the audience, who were very well aware of how hard the economic crisis had hit *Dagbladet*. No Norwegian newspaper had experienced a more dramatic drop in both circulation and turnover than *Dagbladet* during the previous years; no newspaper had been obliged to let so many newsroom staffers go. Anne Aasheim didn't seem to care.

"Our everyday life is all about crisis", she continued. "However, I have been a media executive for 20 years now and I must say, it's more fun today than ever before!"

Some members of the audience looked at each other with slightly raised eyebrows. More *fun* today? Was she joking? Had it come to a point where the challenges of keeping a newspaper alive were so massive that the only way to keep one's head above water was to laugh about it – to treat it like a joke? Or was the position Anne Aasheim took this grey October day in 2009 a reflection of what might be considered the only feasible solution for a struggling newspaper: to treat the crisis like a unique opportunity to create change?

Anne Aasheim soon revealed what she had in mind. She flipped up a PowerPoint slide that read: "The media crisis has given the media companies a new opportunity to pounce on alternative innovation and to question established truths". She then said:

"When the crisis becomes big enough, you no longer just mend things. You tear everything apart, and then you reconstruct it. We are now searching for the power to introduce disruptive innovation. It's going to be a cut-throat competition to have the greatest power of innovation".

Then she smiled before exclaiming: "And we're going to win that competition!"

Three months later, Anne Aasheim resigned as editor-in-chief of *Dagbladet*.

By the end of the first decade of the new millennium, many news companies around the world were in a similar position as the Norwegian tabloid newspaper *Dagbladet*. And as was the case for Anne Aasheim, *Dagbladet*'s editor-in-chief, many editors and news company owners were torn between competing discourses related to how to frame and tackle the situation. A discourse of *crisis* was among the most prevailing. The news industry was in a (self-perceived) state of crisis caused by financial disarray, new ways of distributing news that drew audiences away from legacy news companies, and an increasing decline in the public's trust in news. Simultaneously, there was a discourse of *technological optimism* having a strong hold on the industry. This discourse proclaimed that all the possibilities of new technology and digital culture in general would work in favour of journalism. And finally, a discourse of *innovation*, in which finding new ways of producing, distributing, and consuming news were seen as key to the continued success of the news industry. These three, partly competing, discourses were often present simultaneously, as they were for the *Dagbladet* editor when she gave her speech in October 2009. And they are still dominating the industry as we have entered the third decade of the new millennium.

What is interesting to us is how these three discourses have found their way into digital journalism studies as a research field and how they embed certain normative understandings of journalism and its development in digital times. Digital journalism studies has been preoccupied with crisis, technological optimism, and innovation in an *empirical* sense, implying that much research has investigated the actual state of crisis, technological optimism, and/or innovation. And digital journalism studies has been preoccupied with crisis, technological optimism, and innovation in a *discursive* sense, implying that the perspectives and ways of seeing the world embedded in these discourses have been adopted as presuppositions in the research. It is in such research, when scholars take crisis, technological optimism, or the benefits of innovation for granted – as givens that journalism in digital times must adhere to – that digital journalism studies becomes normative in ways that are hidden and problematic.

We will get back to the discourse of innovation in the next sub-section. In this sub-section we will take a closer look at the research related to the two discourses that deal with future predictions, the discourse of crisis and the discourse of technological optimism, and we will see how they both empirically and discursively construct digital journalism in normative ways.

6.1.1 Digital journalism studies and the discourse of crisis

First, we will look at how the discourse of crisis has travelled from industry to research. A substantial number of scholarly publications focusing on journalism include the word "crisis", even if the phrase "crisis journalism", which signals research on crisis journalism as a beat and not the crisis *of* journalism, is excluded. During the 20 first years of the 21 [st] century, Google Scholar returns 270,130 results for the Boolean search term "journalism" and "crisis" (excluding "crisis journalism"). A similar search for just the term "journalism" returns 947,100 results. In other words; 29 percent of the research found through Google Scholar on journalism includes the word "crisis", thereby suggesting that the discourse of crisis is prominent in journalism studies. Moreover, as illustrated in Figure 6.1, the dominance of "crisis" in journalism research increased substantially during the years 2008 (21 percent) to 2018 (49 percent), in the decade following the financial crisis.

We should not put too much emphasis on such a Google Scholar search exercise. The fact that the word "crisis" appears in a scholarly publication about journalism does not mean that the publication is marked by a discourse of crisis. For instance, a publication could discuss "crisis" in a critical fashion, like Chyi, Lewis & Zheng's (2012) analysis of how

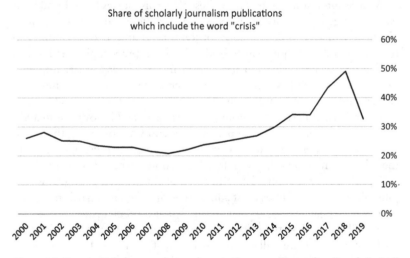

Figure 6.1 Google Scholar search on the search terms "journalism" and "crisis" (excluding "crisis journalism") and how the result compares to a similar Google Scholar search on just the word "journalism".

Note: The search was conducted in January 2020.

newspapers themselves covered the newspaper "crisis". However, the importance of the word crisis in scholarly publications about journalism during the 2000s indicates an increased significance of the discourse of crisis to both journalism studies and digital journalism studies. This discourse has many dimensions. Nielsen (2016) breaks it down to an *economic* crisis caused by the seemingly impossibilities of making revenue on online outlets for the legacy news companies; a *professional* crisis marked by the blurring of boundaries between journalism and other kinds of professional work; and a crisis of *confidence* marked by the public's increasing distrust in news. Zelizer (2015) argues the challenges to journalism normally framed as a crisis have many dimensions: a *political* dimension (news is under threat from both the left and right side of politics); *economic* (the collapse of old business models); a *moral* dimension (too many scandals and violations of ethical standards in journalism); an *occupational* dimension (traditional norms and values of journalism no longer hold); and a *technological* dimension (digital, social media make visible the authoritative voice of journalism and its reluctance to respond to calls for transparency).

No doubt, these dimensions all reflect real challenges that have caused severe problems for journalism in many countries. It is a well-established fact that journalism in many countries has suffered financially across recent decades, predominantly because the advertisement-based business model of the printed press is not viable in a digital economy increasingly dominated by big platform companies like Google, Amazon, and Facebook (see chapter 4, section 4.1 for a more in-depth discussion of this). Similarly, empirical studies show that the public's trust in news has declined in many countries (see Newman et al., 2019 and earlier Reuters Institute Digital News Reports), and that anticipations of audience participation and transparency in journalism has increased, probably as a result of a cultural shift reflected by digital, social media. Studies also indicate that these anticipations have not been met by journalism (Singer et al., 2011) and that the boundaries of journalism as both practice and profession are blurring (see, for instance, the collection of research essays in Carlson & Lewis, 2015).

In other words: there are no problems, nor necessarily any normative assumptions lurking in the background, with the attention digital journalism studies pays to these challenges. In fact, one might argue that digital journalism scholars would neglect their core responsibilities if they did not address the concerns of the industry and the challenges facing journalism in digital times. However, there are some potential problems with how researchers might discursively frame these challenges. Adopting the word "crisis" for any of these challenges irrevocably frames them with a high degree of acute seriousness, with a specific urgency that places the here-and-now of journalism in a disruptive relationship with both the past and the future. The discourse of crisis pushes scholars into a position in which the past is viewed as an endurable phase with manageable challenges, the present is perceived as a decisive moment at which massive changes must take place, and the future is seen as a time marked by greater uncertainty than ever, a time that relies entirely on journalism's ability to take drastic measures here and now. According to Zelizer (2015, p. 892), the word crisis becomes "a way of lexically editing from the picture alternative realities in order to frame the subject of address in simplistic, familiar, and strategically useful ways", which in turn help "turn murky and troublesome challenges into a controllable phenomenon that can be identified, articulated, managed, and ultimately gotten rid of". The discourse of crisis therefore adds an alarmist attitude to the challenges facing journalism while at the same time interpreting them in a reductionist and simplistic manner.

This discursive construction of the challenges facing journalism in digital times therefore has some significant normative underpinnings: First, it pushes a skewed relationship with *time*, in which the significance of the present is overestimated. Digital journalism studies in general is marked by a bias towards the contemporary, not only because it investigates predominantly the present, but also, as we pointed to in chapter 5, section 5.3, because to an excessive extent, it relies on references to contemporary research. Consequently, digital journalism studies risks treating current events as both more significant and more unique than they are, since lessons from the past are not taken into account in a satisfactory manner.

Second, the crisis discourse creates a bias towards *space* (or more precisely: geography) in digital journalism studies (Zelizer, 2015). The discourse pushes a universal understanding of the state of journalism, which implies that there is one crisis in journalism, in singular terms, a crisis that knows no border or cultural diversity. This, of course, is not true. First of all, journalism is not in crisis in all parts of the world. When many scholars speak of the crisis in journalism, what this is often understood to mean are the challenges that journalism has faced in predominantly Western democracies during the 21st century. Imposing such Western ways of conceptualising journalism has been a problem in journalism studies in general, a problem, which might lead to dangerous presuppositions and over-generalisations of findings (Esser & Hanitzsch, 2012). A growing body of comparative research in recent years has shown that the differences between journalistic cultures around the global are quite large, and that national factors much more than cross-national or even global trends explain variances in journalism in different cultures (Hanitzsch, 2020). For example, whereas the printed press in most Western countries indeed has been in a steep decline in the 21 st century, the opposite is true in a country like India, which has seen a substantial growth in print circulation and advertising at the same time as digital news media has also grown (Aneez, Chattapadhyay, Parthasarathi, & Nielsen, 2016).

There are not only differences between journalism in Western democracies and other parts of the world; there are also significant difference between Western democracies (Nielsen, 2016). For instance, the alleged crisis in trust in journalism varies greatly between countries like Finland, Denmark, and Portugal, where people still (in 2019) have quite high trust in the news media, and countries like France and Greece where the public's trust in news is much lower (Newman et al., 2019, sec. 1, p. 19). In addition, regarding the economic state of the news media and people's willingness to pay for news, there are major differences. In Norway and Sweden, digital revenues are rising significantly, while the news industry in other countries has severe problems. Twenty-six percent of Norwegians have an ongoing subscription to a news medium, while only 6 percent of Germans and Italians have the same (Newman et al., 2019, sec. 2, p. 33).

6.1.2 Digital journalism studies and the discourse of technological optimism

Similar to the discourse of crisis, the discourse of technological optimism is often rooted in an assumed causal relationship between technology and journalism. But where this causal relationship predicts the doomsday of journalism within the discourse of crisis, the discourse of technological optimism envisions a future utopia in which technologies change journalism for the better. Mosco (2004) has argued that such mythical discursive powers have dominated the relationships between media, communication, and technology throughout history. The telephone, radio, television, and computer have all been surrounded by such revolutionary myths, either pessimistic or optimistic. The 1990s saw several publications in which authors were profoundly optimistic on behalf of the future of journalism in new, digital media. Boczkowski (2004) and Domingo (2006) argued that such early future-predictions were driven by technological determinism and that research into digital (or online) journalism during the first decade of its existence was partly paralysed by what Domingo (2006) labelled "utopias of online journalism". These utopias were especially related to how hypertext, multimedia, and interactivity would foster innovative approaches that would revolutionise journalism.

These three concepts – hypertext, multimedia, and interactivity – were central to how the discourse of technological optimism affected digital journalism studies up until 2010, and even later (Steensen, 2011b).

Even though the research into hypertextual, interactive, and multimedia features of digital journalism has become richer and more nuanced over the years, the discourse of technological optimism has survived as a normative premise for much of it, alongside, or as a counterpoint to, the competing discourse of crisis. The problems with this discourse of technological optimism are 1) its inclination to be driven by technological determinism; 2) that the significance of technological skills and assets is overestimated; and 3) that it is based on the assumption that new technology will benefit journalism. Regarding technological determinism, there is no doubt that a technology-centric approach to studying digital journalism risks adopting a causal relationship between technology and practice, in which technology is the one factor that forces change upon journalistic practice. Influences from sciences and technology studies and ethnographic approaches to investigate the relationships between technology and practice have, however, provided much needed nuance to the ways in which this relationship is understood (see chapter 5, section 5.2.2). However, since digital journalism as practice quite often promotes understandings of the relationship between technology and society in line with technological determinism (Post & Crone, 2015), there is always the risk that digital journalism scholars will follow.

The second problem of overestimating the significance of technological skills and assets implies that much research, even though it may be based on a nuanced understanding of the relationship between technology and practice, risks placing too much emphasis on technology. The importance of technological skills and assets for journalists in digital times has been highlighted by many, but some studies indicate that the *perceived* need for skills related to digital technology is much higher than what is actually needed in the everyday practice of digital journalism (Himma-Kadakas & Palmiste, 2019), and that too much emphasis on technical skills might overshadow the important basic skills in journalism, related for instance to critical thinking and accountability (Ferrucci, 2018). Moreover, in in their review of a decade of research on social media and journalism, Lewis and Molyneux (2018) argue that much of this research has been based on the assumption that social media matter more than other factors for journalism, an assumption, they argue, which is not necessarily true.

The third problem of taking for granted that new technology could benefit journalism is also found to be a problem by Lewis and Molyneux (2018) in their review of social media and journalism research. They conclude that the research suffers from the normative assumptions that social media is a net positive for journalism. As recent developments and research have demonstrated – and as we discussed in chapter 4, section 4.1.2 – this is a problematic assumption. The assumed benefits of social media for journalism, like transparency, reaching new audiences, breaking news faster, greater variance in sources, more audience participation and engagement, have not materialised in the ways assumed by early research. Moreover, problems like the harassment of journalists through social media (Chen et al., 2018), the spread of fake news and other forms of disinformation through social media (Allcott & Gentzkow, 2017), and other forms of "dark participation" (Quandt, 2018) are indeed signs that social media are not necessarily positive for journalism. In addition, the effect social media have had on the stream of revenue coming from advertisements for journalism tip the scale even further to the negative side for journalism. Some even argue that social media represent "the single biggest challenge facing journalism today" (Crilley & Gillespie, 2019, p. 173).

6.2 Digital journalism studies and the discourse of innovation

As was the case with the discourse of crisis, the discourse of innovation is quite dominant in journalism studies during the first 20 years of the 21st century if we look at publications found through Google Scholar searches. A search on "journalism" and "innovation" returns 179,750 results for the years 2000–2019, which amounts to 19 percent of all journalism publications found when searching for only "journalism". And similar to the discourse of crisis, the discourse of innovation seems to have increased in significance. As is visible in Figure 6.2, the popularity of "innovation" in Google Scholar search results on journalism grew steadily from 13 percent of all journalism publications in 2008 to 34 percent in 2018, before falling slightly in popularity in 2019. In other words: one third of all scholarly publications mentioning "journalism" found in Google Scholar and published in 2018 also included the word "innovation".

Innovation research tends to emphasise newness and change. Whether it is a new idea, a new technology, a new commodity or a new combination of existing ideas, technologies, or commodities, it is the newness and its consequences that are under scrutiny. Newness and change are in other words integral parts of innovation as discourse. This discourse also emphasises structural factors such as technology and economy as drivers of change (Steensen, 2013), and it is therefore linked to the discourse of technological optimism discussed above. Posetti (2018) describes this

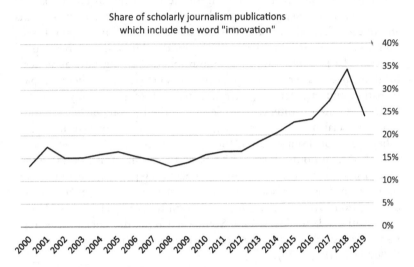

Share of scholarly journalism publications
which include the word "innovation"

Figure 6.2 Google Scholar search on the terms "journalism" and "innovation" and how
the result compares to a similar Google Scholar search on just the word
"journalism".

Note: The search was conducted in January 2020.

link between the innovation discourse and technological optimism as the
"Shiny Things Syndrome", a syndrome which may distract journalism
from its core functions, according to the international journalism innovation leaders Posetti interviewed for her study.

6.2.1 The newness bias

The "Shiny Things Syndrome", or the fascination with "shiny, new
things" as Kueng (2017) calls it, is related to the newness aspect of the
discourse of innovation. Even though both Posetti's and Kueng's findings are related to warnings from the industry itself, the syndrome also
applies to digital journalism studies. Like journalists and editors, researchers are drawn to new, shiny things. As we have discussed earlier in this
chapter and also elsewhere in this book (see for instance chapter 2, section 2.2.2) new technologies and their potential impact on journalism is a
recurring theme in digital journalism studies. However, the emphasis on
newness in digital journalism studies goes beyond a fascination with new
technology. For instance, the increased popularity of digital ethnography,
both in newsrooms and beyond (see Robinson & Metzler, 2016 for an

overview), bears with it some methodological problems long recognised in anthropology, for example. This problem concerns an embedded bias towards behaviourism. When conducting ethnographic research in a newsroom, for example, the researcher is automatically drawn to activities, and especially those activities that stand out, that have something new, not previously observed, to them. Engelman (1960) labelled this phenomenon the "activity bias" and argued that the emphasis on "overt activities" in ethnographic research consequently "disregards experience, negates the obvious complexities of internal behavioural dynamics, and reduces the behaviour system to an automaton" (1960, p. 158). Even though ethnography as a method has developed strategies to include experiences and nuanced understandings of the actors being observed, the bias towards overt activities is difficult to overcome, simply because an observation-based research project that does not find something new, and only confirms what is already known, is not going to attract any attention. This, of course, is not only a problem with ethnographic research. In the natural sciences, experiments are rarely published if negative and – because of an emphasis on novelty – such studies are rarely replicated.

This bias towards things and activities that seemingly stand out, the newness bias, affect digital journalism studies in numerous ways. The application of Actor-Network Theory (ANT) and other socio-technical approaches to researching digital journalism (see chapter 5, section 5.2.2) is one example. The benefit of such approaches is that they make visible the importance of non-human actors like technology in how digital journalism is practiced and developed. However, ANT and similar approaches can lead to an overestimation of non-human actors like technology, simply because humans and non-humans belong to different ontologies and therefore can't be juxtaposed (Vandenberghe, 2002). Vandenberghe argues that such approaches misjudge the power relation between humans and non-humans in their "fetish"-like preoccupation with objects and artefacts: "[h]owever humans are inter-connected with non-humans, at the end of the day, it is humans who encounter non-humans and endow them with meaning, use or value" (2002, p. 55). There is therefore a risk that non-human actors and actants are ascribed too much meaning and power.

Another example of the newness bias is the tendency to overestimate both the significance and the newness of the things that stand out in the research findings. The things that stand out become bigger and more important because we as researchers choose to focus our attention on them, not because they necessarily play a more important role in news production. The first author of this book has been a victim of this bias when he led a research project on online sports journalism

(Steensen, 2011a). He found that "social cohesion" was a new ideal for sports journalists who live-blogged soccer games, but he overestimated the significance of this ideal to the professional identity of sports journalists and failed to recognise that this ideal is not new to journalism. Even in Boczkowski's (2004) influential ethnographic study of digital initiatives in online newsrooms we find examples of such overestimations. One of the initiatives Boczkowski analysed was *The Houston Chronicle*'s Virtual Voyager project, which was an advanced multimedia project in the late 1990s, probably one of the most advanced and innovative multimedia projects produced by an online newspaper at the time. And yet, after analysing the case, Boczkowski (2004, p. 138) argued: "Regarding more general analytical matters, the story of the Virtual Voyager allows us to go deeper into the material dimension of online editorial work". Such an analytical move from the particular to the general is problematic, simply because Virtual Voyager was an exception. It was the extreme case.

6.2.2 *The problems with change and how to deal with them*

Strongly connected with newness, *change* is the other important aspect of the discourse of innovation. The significance of change to digital journalism studies is expressed in the introductory chapters of the two recently published handbooks of digital journalism studies. Eldridge II and Franklin (2017, p. 4) argue that digital journalism studies "can be understood through the ways it has embraced unclear definitional boundaries around journalism as it has experienced radical change in the past few decades". Witschge, Anderson, Domingo, and Hermida (2016a, p. 2) argue that digital journalism studies "need to address changing contexts and new practices, need to reconsider theories and develop research strategies". Ahva and Steensen (2017) argue that digital journalism studies has evolved from viewing change as a revolution to change as deconstruction, implying that digital journalism studies today is preoccupied with deconstructing previously established notions of what journalism is.

Change is indeed an important aspect of digital journalism studies in general, perhaps even its fundamental building block. And yet, or perhaps precisely because of this, the importance of change and innovation is often taken for granted, for instance in statements like "[t]he only constant in contemporary journalism is change, and innovation is essential to the survival of the news industry" (Posetti, 2018, p. 8). When researchers put much emphasis on the things that change and treat change and innovation as constants, there is always the risk that the things that do *not* change are neglected and that descriptions of change become more important than, for example, figuring out the deeper relations between journalism and society. In the words of Peters and Carlson (2019, p. 639): "one of the dangers in placing change above solidity is the increased difficulty of moving from the surface to engage in deeper social questions".

The discourse of innovation will emphasise newness over sameness; change over continuity; young over old, and – in relation to media and journalism especially – digital over analogue. The challenge for us as researchers who are interested in the developments in journalism is not to forget the things that stay the same, the things that are old and the things that are analogue. But even though we are well aware of this, it is difficult not to get caught up in the discourse of innovation. One way of balancing the biases of the discourse of innovation is to consider the potential counter-discourses embedded in the perspectives of *transformation* and *practice*, argues Steensen (2013). The transformation perspective can complement innovation research by drawing attention to historical developments and by pointing to the importance of genres and thus the social function of texts to developments in digital journalism. Journalism relies to a great extent on genres, implying that journalistic communication must be recognised as such by the audience in order for the communication to be successful. The only way of achieving such communicative success is by relying on genres, understood as recognisable text formats with specific discursive features that occur in repeated social situations (Miller, 1984). Genres are in other words conservative, since they rely on previous communicative experiences and established conventions. They do not easily change. Remembering this might help in counter-balancing the normative implications of the innovation discourse.

The practice perspective can complement both the transformation and innovation perspectives by stressing the importance of micro-sociological relations to developments in digital journalism, and by pointing out that the journalistic institutions of today "allow for a different kind of interplay between structure and agency, where agency may pave, or block, the way for innovation diffusion unbound by external macro-societal factors" (Steensen, 2013, pp. 56–57).

6.3 Concluding remarks

Normativity influences digital journalism studies in many ways. We have chosen to focus on three discourses, which we argue influence much of digital journalism studies in normative ways: the discourses of crisis, technological optimism, and innovation. This focus allowed us to look at some of the ways in which normativity is often hidden in digital journalism studies in relation to topics that have great importance to the field. We do not argue that normativity should have no place in digital journalism studies. The point we would like to stress is that normativity is more common than one perhaps would think. It is important to increase the awareness about such hidden normativity in digital journalism studies in order to see how it affects research and how it can be either made more transparent or countered by framing the research with perspectives from other, contrasting discourses.

What we have not discussed in this chapter, is the ways in which digital journalism studies *should* be normative, perhaps to a greater extent than it is today. Some of the major societal challenges as we enter the 2020s, like climate change, the diffusion of disinformation, and political extremism and polarisation, have impacts on digital journalism and thereby also on digital journalism studies. For instance, we think that normative assumptions should underlie any assessment of how digital technologies are used to spread alternative "news" realities, misinform certain publics, create polarisation, foster distrust in research, and so forth. As digital journalism sees the rise of alternate news sites, which fundamentally challenge traditional understandings of what journalism is for, its role in democratic societies and the line between ethical and opportunistic producers of public affairs, normativity may – in fact – be central to how research questions should be generated. Digital journalism studies should not take a neutral stand regarding what is journalism and what is not. Moreover, digital journalism studies should seek, as one of its missions, to further develop practices of journalism suited to tackle major societal challenges, perhaps in line with emerging practise like solutions journalism (McIntyre, 2019) or constructive journalism (McIntyre & Gyldensted, 2017).

Note

1 The scene opening this sub-section was originally published in a longer version in Steensen (2010, pp. 1–3). All quotes, which originally were spoken in Norwegian, are translated by the authors.

7 The methodologies

How digital journalism is researched

Research methods are tied to theory. The bridge between them is the research question you ask, which on the one side is connected with the theoretical assumptions you make, and on the other determines which methods you can apply. If we return to the imagined research project we introduced chapter 5, the one involving the fictional news company *The Daily Times*, its Snapchat initiative, and a tech start-up, we can identify how the many research questions that could be asked in this case would require different methods. For instance, a research question like *to what degree does the case change what it means to be a journalist* would require **interviews**, either structured in the form of **surveys**, semi-structured in the form of qualitative, in-depth interviews, or unstructured as part of **ethnographic field work**. If your research question is *to what degree the new product manages to get new audiences interested in public affairs*, you would have to apply some kind of audience research, like **focus group interviews**, **experiments**, **analysis of the digital footprints** audiences leave behind when consuming news, or **Q-methodology** to analyse the media repertoires of individuals. If you are more interested in whether the new initiative allows for new and diverse voices to be heard in journalism, you would probably want to utilise quantitative or qualitative **content analysis** of the texts produced in order to trace sources. If you want to go into more detail and understand not only what kinds of voices are represented, but *how* they are represented, you would have to conduct some kind of qualitative text analysis, like **critical discourse analysis**, **rhetoric analysis**, **frame analysis**, or similar methods of text analysis. If you are more interested in the communicative aspects of the journalism produced and how it relates to other forms of communication, you could perform a **genre analysis**. But if you want to find out how the journalism produced on Snapchat impacts the information network this social medium constitutes and is part of, you may want to apply some kind of **data analytics, network analysis,** or similar, more technically oriented methods. If your research question is broad, like *how the case might affect journalism's position and role in society,* you would probably use several of the above mentioned methods and others in a **mixed-methods approach** and you would probably like to compare this one case with other cases in a **multiple case study.**

The possibilities are in other words almost endless. The interdisciplinary nature of digital journalism studies means that the field applies a wide range of methods from many different disciplines and fields. A question is, however, to what degree the field has advanced its methodological approaches beyond the common methods traditionally found in journalism studies in order to address the specific characteristics of the *digital* in digital journalism. In their introduction to a special issue of *Digital Journalism* on research methods, Karlsson and Sjøvaag (2016b, p. 1) argue it has not: "While journalism theory has indeed been advanced, the same can unfortunately not be said about methodologies used in journalism research".

This chapter will *not* provide a complete account of all methods used in digital journalism studies – such an endeavour would require a book of its own. Instead, we will focus on the methods that recently have become available for researchers in the field and the ones that are important in order to answer research questions related to the themes and topics that shape the field: technology, platforms, and audiences (see chapters 3 and 4). In other words, the chapter will focus on 1) digital methods suited to advance content analysis and the analysis of digital journalism in networked spaces; 2) digital ethnography suited to analyse digital journalism in and beyond the newsroom; and 3) methods suited to analyse how audiences interact with news. First, however, we will take a look at what our analysis of articles in the journal *Digital Journalism* can tell us about commonalities in methods applied.

In it is important to note from the very start that methods are not only tied to theory; they are also tied to the sociology of knowledge. Different methods embed, to a certain extent, different ways of assessing what counts as valid knowledge. Choosing a method therefore involves epistemological decisions. A recurring theme throughout this chapter is how new technology and the availability of digital data, both big and small, create not only new methodological opportunities for digital journalism studies, but also some potential biases and epistemological challenges related to the kinds of knowledge that numbers can produce and the significance of that knowledge.

authors pay equal attention to theory and methodology. However, some of the keywords we have classified as belonging to the *theory* thematic cluster, like "discourse", "framing", and "ANT" (actor-network theory), are commonly also understood as methodologies. If these where to be included in Table 7.1 they would be placed quite high up since the keyword "discourse" occurred in 11 articles, "ANT" in 5, and "framing" in 4.

As is visible in Table 7.1, content analysis is by far the most popular method in digital journalism studies judged by the degree to which authors who publish in *Digital Journalism* signal their methods in keywords. Surveys and interviews are also popular approaches, as are comparative methodology, which echoes the increased popularity of comparative research in journalism studies in general (Hanitzsch, 2020).

A few interesting observations can be made concerning the keywords listed in Table 7.1. First, most methods are only mentioned once or twice. This does not necessarily mean that these methods or methodological concepts are applied on only one or two occasions in the research published in *Digital Journalism*, since they can have been applied without being listed as keywords. Yet, it signals that methodological diversity and perhaps also experimentation is part of digital journalism studies, a point which probably is reflected by the fact that "methods" in itself is quite a popular keyword. Second, quite a few of the keywords refer to statistical methods: topic modelling, LDA (Latent Dirichlet Allocation, which is a type of topic modelling), regression, multilevel analysis, structural equation modelling, and topic detection. This signals that the "quantitative turn" in journalism (Coddington, 2015) applies also to digital journalism studies, a point we will get back to later. However, even though such statistical keywords might signal a turn towards computational methods, they are not used very often, and we don't find many examples of computational methods used in digital journalism studies, thereby suggesting that manual methods are still the norm in the field.

Third, methods traditionally identified with the humanities do not occur very often; "text analysis" is for instance only listed once as a keyword. This is a point recognised also in Steensen and colleagues' (2019) qualitative analysis of 95 articles published in *Digital Journalism*, in which they found that 13 of the 95 articles applied qualitative, humanistic methods and that the authors applying methods related to qualitative text and discourse analysis "often seemed to do so without applying the research tools commonly associated with humanistic text analysis" (2019, p. 331).

If we look at the references to methods literature in the articles published in *Digital Journalism*, we find several references to the methods' journals *Communication Methods and Measures*, *Field Methods*, *International Journal of Social Research Methodology*, *Sociological Methods & Research*, and

Behavior Research Methods. The popularity of these journals is a further indication of the dominance of social science methods and perspectives in digital journalism studies, as we discussed in chapter 5. Among the methods' monographs or edited volumes referenced, Krippendorf's (2004 and other editions) *Content Analysis* is the most popular, in addition to other content analysis literature. Yin's (2003) *Case Study Research* is also cited quite many times, while books like *Social Research Methods* (Bryman, 2012), *Digital Methods* (R. Rogers, 2013), *Audience Research Methodology* (Patriarche, Bilandzic, Linaa Jensen, & Jurišić, 2014), *Q Methodology: A Sneak Preview* (Van Exel & De Graaf, 2005), and *Methods of Critical Discourse Analysis* (Wodak & Meyer, 2001) are all cited in more than one article.

If we look at articles that predominantly discuss methodology published *in* the journal *Digital Journalism*, we find quite a few. Sixteen articles published in the journal aim primarily at discussing research methods, most of them published in a special issue titled *Rethinking Research Methods in an Age of Digital Journalism* (issue 1, 2016). About half of these 16 articles discuss various kinds of computational methods, thus signalling that much of the methodological development within digital journalism studies is related to how technology can advance research designs. We will look more closely into this in the next section.

7.2 Numbers, metrics, and computational methods

In their introduction to the special issue of *Digital Journalism* on research methods in an age of digital journalism, Karlsson and Sjøvaag (2016b, p. 1) lament the lack of methodological innovation in digital journalism studies "despite the many methodological challenges that follow from the characteristics of digital media and digital journalism". They argue that as the object of study changes, old methods of investigating it may no longer be feasible. Even though methods like content analysis, interviews, and surveys have not lost their significance and still will generate valuable insights into various aspects of digital journalism, the general emphasis on datafication in journalism, and in societies at large (Van Dijck, 2014), has opened new opportunities and necessities for *what* to analyse and *how* to do it.

Concerning the *what*: one core characteristic of digital journalism is, as we have discussed earlier, especially in chapter 4, section 4.1, its entanglement in information networks, dominated by social media platforms. Analysing such networks, and journalism's role in them, might require new methods. A second characteristic, which we discussed in chapters 3 and 4, is the ways in which numbers and metrics have become pivotal in monitoring (and capitalising on) audience behaviour in digital journalism. Analysing aspects of this development might also require new research methods. And finally, a third characteristic is that as data analytics and computational methods become more common in practices of digital journalism, considering how this "quantitative turn" (Coddington, 2015) affects digital journalism also becomes important.

Concerning the *how* to research the three *whats* above: an increasingly large pool of computational methods and techniques can be used to collect and analyse data on a wide range of topics related to the production, distribution, and consumption of journalism (see overviews in Bruns, 2016; Larsson, Sjøvaag, Karlsson, Stavelin, & Moe, 2016). No doubt, methods developed within computer science and computational linguistics can be used for instance to automate content analysis, to analyse information networks, and to analyse news use and audience metrics. We will return to the latter in section 7.4. Here we will first look more closely at the developments in content analysis in digital journalism studies, before we discuss computational analysis of information networks, and if there are any potential problems with such methods.

7.2.1 Advancing content analysis in digital journalism studies

Already in the very first issue of *Digital Journalism*, Flaounas and colleagues (2013) argued that the emerging field of computational social science had much to offer digital journalism studies, especially related to advancing the method of content analysis. The article presents the findings from a content analysis of 2.5 million articles in online newspapers, and a main purpose is to demonstrate "how automated approaches can access both semantic and stylistic properties of content, and therefore how content analysis can be scaled to sizes that were previously unreachable" (2013, p. 102). To achieve such a scaling, the researchers used techniques of data mining, machine learning, and natural language processing.

Such large-scale, automated content analysis have been used to analyse for example news formats in all articles published online by the Norwegian public broadcaster NRK during one year (Sjøvaag & Stavelin, 2012); agenda divergence in Russian and Ukrainian news in the course of the Ukrainian crisis 2013–2014 (Koltsova & Pashakhin, 2019); the perception and the conceptualisation of the term "fake news" in news media in 20 countries over a period of eight years (Cunha, Magno, Caetano, Teixeira, & Almeida, 2018); and gender representation in 2.3 million articles from more than 950 online news outlets (Jia, Lansdall-Welfare, Sudhahar, Carter, & Cristianini, 2016), to name but a few. Automated, large-scale content analysis has also been used with aims that span way beyond digital journalism studies, like Lansdall-Welfare et al. (2017), who analyse cultural and social transitions in the British society through an analysis of 14 percent of all articles published in regional British newspapers over a time period of 150 years. Moreover, Broussard (2015) shows how automated, large-scale content analysis can aid the practice of journalism, especially investigative reporting.

Applying automated, large-scale content analysis methods is not easy, and it often requires interdisciplinary research teams comprising advanced skills in computer science, computational linguistics, and/or statistics in addition to journalism studies. Boumans and Trilling (2016) offer a toolkit of various approaches and techniques related to automated content analysis of digital journalism, as do Günther and Quandt (2016), who offer a step-by-step guide on how to perform such analysis. In this guide, the authors demonstrate the complexity of the process and warn that techniques developed within disciplines very different from the social sciences cannot be adopted without careful preparation, simply because "computers do not understand texts the way human coders can, and are only as good as the algorithms they perform" (2016, p. 86).

In addition to the problems of applying techniques from computer science to digital journalism studies, there are also problems with applying principles of traditional content analysis to computational and automated content analysis. For example, Karlsson and Sjøvaag (2016a, p. 178) argue there are some problems with using established categories of content analysis to analyse emerging forms of digital journalism, since the method and the ways in which it traditionally has been applied in journalism studies is "grounded in space/time assumptions that resonate with analogue media, in general, and print media, in particular". Karlsson and Sjøvaag therefore suggest two novel approaches to content analysis of digital journalism: a big data approach, similar to those discussed above, and what they label "liquid content analysis", which allows for tracking the life cycle of a news item, which in digital media is not fixed, like in a printed newspaper, but appears in many different iterations and is intertwined with other current and past news. This liquidity of digital journalism points to the increasing networked nature of contemporary information flows, of which journalism is part. The next section will look specifically at methods suited to analyse such networks.

7.2.2 Computational methods and analysis of information networks

The increased significance of platform companies and the diversification of means for distributing information in contemporary media landscapes have boosted an interest in the ways in which information from various sources diffuses in societies. Phrases like "information networks" (e.g., Guo & McCombs, 2015), "news networks" (e.g., Domingo et al., 2015), and "news ecosystem" (e.g., C. W. Anderson, 2016) have become an integrated part of digital journalism studies, implying that news and journalism in digital times are increasingly seen as parts of larger information systems involving many actors and actants both proprietary and non-proprietary to journalistic institutions. Analysing such information and news networks and journalism's role in them has therefore become an important task for digital journalism studies. Typical examples include analysis of how news related to a specific topic or event travels across or between various platforms. For reasons we will get back to in the next section, much of this research has focused on the relationship between journalism and Twitter, like Wang and Guo's (2018) inter-media agenda setting analysis of how the discussion about genetically modified mosquitoes was framed in news media and on Twitter; Malik and Pfeffer's (2016) analysis of the dominance of news organisations on Twitter; and Steensen and Eide's (2019) analysis of news flows between traditional, journalistic media and a national Twittersphere during a terrorist attack.

A common methodological approach in such research is to analyse *hyperlinks*. Hyperlinks carry meaning beyond their technical materiality in digital journalism, as they are associated with values like interactivity, transparency, credibility, and diversity (De Maeyer & Holton, 2016). Hyperlinks can therefore be analysed in order to assess, for instance, when, where, and how often online content travels across different platforms, or how various information networks are structured. The advantage of hyperlinks is that they are unique identifiers, which stay the same across different platforms. Analysing a selection of hyperlinks across platforms can be done manually by using platform-spesific search tools, but if the aim is to analyse a large selection of hyperlinks or identify all hyperlinks on a spesific platform or in a specific network in a given time period, then computational methods and innovative approaches are required.

An illustrative example is Sjøvaag et al.'s (2019) study of hyperlinks in Scandinavian online news sites. In this study, the researchers analysed 22 million hyperlinks from 658 Scandinavian news websites in order to assess the structural properties of the Scandinavian media system. They wrote a script that collected hyperlinks from all the websites and stored the internal links in one place and the external links in a database. Seventy-nine million external links were stored, of which 22 million were links between the 658 news websites. These 22 million hyperlinks where then analysed using the Gephi software, including a geolayout plugin, and the Python package NetwrokX (Sjøvaag et al., 2019, p. 514). In other words, the methods used required advanced skills in computers science, and the research team was interdisciplinary, consisting of journalism scholars and computer scientists.

7.2.3 Problems with big data computational methods

Analysing big data sets with computational methods have implications beyond the research questions asked and answers found. "Big data" does not only contribute new empirical and analytical opportunities; it also comes with a certain discursive baggage implying a certain epistemological normativity related to what constitutes valuable knowledge. Embedded in this discourse is often an assumption that the bigger the data, the better the research, and consequently that the more data one can analyse, the more accurate and valuable is the knowledge produced (Boyd & Crawford, 2012). Such assumptions not only risk devaluating research not based on big data analysis, they also risk promoting uninteresting research simply because the value might be perceived as lying in the possibilities of capturing big data and not in the knowledge that the data potentially can produce. However, big data can definitely produce valuable knowledge, as the examples above illustrate. The point is that as with all other research approaches, the value of the knowledge produced is only as good as the value of the research questions asked, independent of the size of the data analysed. Digital journalism scholars should therefore make sure that they have interesting questions to ask before they embark on analysis of big data.

This potential big data problem is not the only problem computational methods might cause. For instance, analysing hyperlinks can be problematic because links are quite often stand-ins for what one really wants to investigate. As argued by Finkelstein (2008), analysing hyperlinks presupposes that the links are carriers of relevant content and that it is possible to measure the authoritativeness of that content by counting the number of links to it. Analysing hyperlinks is therefore not the same as analysing content, and there is consequently a degree of what we can call *symbolic replaceability* in the kind of hyperlink research that aims at finding answers to questions regarding the content the links refer to. This points to one of several problems with quantitative, automated content analysis and other computational methods in digital journalism studies, namely that texts, both verbal and non-verbal, which ultimately make up the content sought to be analysed, have many qualitative aspects, which will get lost when using quantitative methods. In the words of Karlsson and Sjøvaag (2016a, p. 189):

> When accessing news content as digitally encoded material, we must realize that what we are studying is not news items as they appear on

the screen. Digital news objects cannot be studied in the form that they appear, but must be broken down to enable quantification – to again be aggregated to allow for analysis.

This does not mean that quantitative methods should be avoided when analysing texts, it only means that researchers should be aware what they can actually analyse with such methods. As Grimmer and Stewart (2013, p. 269) pointed out: "All quantitative models of language are wrong – but some are useful". Big data analysis of texts can be useful to detect patterns and structural characteristics of large corpuses of content, but it is not suited to acquire "the deep knowledge and understanding that can be achieved when researchers engage with the units of analysis on a one-to-one basis" (Karlsson & Sjøvaag, 2016a, p. 189). Depending on the research question asked, combining quantitative methods with qualitative analysis could therefore be advisable. Adding automation and machine learning to the quantitative analysis of texts might create additional problems, because the sampling process and partly also the analysis might become invisible to the researcher, like a black box. Acknowledging this problem, Broersma and Harbers (2018) argue that only by making transparent the classification process embedded in machine learning algorithms can researchers employ computational methods in a reliable and valid way.

Another problem related to the breakdown of content to make it feasible to analyse with computational methods, is that the contextual and visual elements of the content disappear from the analysis. Images and layout has always been central elements in journalism, and are so in digital journalism too, but they are difficult to analyse with automated content analysis. However, some researcher have found ways to include visual elements in automated content analysis, like Jia et al. (2016), who analysed gender bias in news, including both words and pictures.

Restrictions on access to data can also constitute a problem for researchers, and push their focus in directions where data can be found instead of where the interesting questions are, much like the joke about the man searching for something lost in a different place than where it was lost simply because the light is better where he searches. Platform companies like Twitter and Facebook have to a large degree commercialised data access, which make it difficult for researchers to analyse the interplay between journalism and such platforms. Third party services like Gnip (Twitter) and CrowdTangle (Facebook and Instagram), which have been acquired by the respective platform companies, provide some access to the platforms' APIs to researchers, but only in a restricted fashion. Full access to all Twitter content (the "firehose" API) has become too costly for most researchers, while CrowdTangle only allows access to public content on Facebook and Instagram, excluding comments. However, since Twitter has allowed access to a smaller portion of its content for free (the "gardenhose" API) and since most Twitter content is public, analysis of content on this platform has dominated much of the social media-related digital journalism research way beyond what the actual significance of the platform would suggest. Digital journalism studies therefore suffers from a Twitter bias, which is illustrated by the fact that "Twitter" is the most frequently mentioned social media company in the platform thematic cluster of keywords we have identified in our analysis of keywords in articles published in *Digital Journalism*. "Twitter" is in fact the third most frequent of all keywords used in *Digital Journalism*. It appears 41 times in the 362 articles published between issue 1, 2013 and issue 4, 2019. By comparison, "Facebook" appears 19 times, even though this social media platform has a much bigger user base and therefore is of much higher significance to digital journalism than Twitter.

7.3 Digital ethnography

The networked nature of the production, distribution, and consumption of digital journalism discussed above also poses some challenges for *ethnographic* research. Participatory observation, the key method used in ethnography, became a forceful approach in journalism studies as part of the classical news production studies during the 1970s, a research tradition which was brought back to popularity at the beginning of the new millennium with influential publications such as Boczkowski (2004), Paterson and Domingo (2008), and later also Domingo and Paterson (2011), Ryfe (2012), Anderson (2013), and Usher (2014), to name but a few. This new wave of ethnographic research sought to understand how the internet and digital technology affected the practices and cultures of news production. Not only was this research pivotal in establishing an understanding of how technology and practice mutually shape one another in newsrooms (see chapter 5, section 5.2.2), it also made apparent that the ethnographic methods of pre-internet news production studies needed revisions in order to be appropriate for studies of modern, digital newsrooms.

We discussed one problem related to digital ethnography in chapter 6, section 6.2.1, namely that this method is associated with an "activity bias" (Engelmann, 1960) which in many cases will favour newness over sameness and change over continuity. However, there are also other problems. First of all – and following from the increasingly networked nature of news production, distribution, and consumption discussed above – modern, digital newsrooms are much less fixed in time and space then their more analogue predecessors. They are scattered across multiple places, platforms, and possibly also organisations, while digital communication technologies collapse the distance between them. In the words of Cottle (2007, p. 9): "With journalists and editors based in different locations but all working on the same story and all able to access, transmit and edit the same news materials clearly this poses considerable challenges to today's ethnographer". A single researcher cannot be several places at the same time. This problem therefore limits the data that one researcher can collect. Having teams of ethnographers present at multiple sites simultaneously can therefore be necessary, but is rarely possible because of the costs involved. However, the discursive practice of news (i.e., the production, distribution, and consumption of news) is no longer limited to the increasingly scattered newsroom. It also involves third-party actors and platforms, like citizen reporters and social media. Capturing the most relevant aspects of news production might therefore mean looking beyond the newsroom and tracing important actors and actants elsewhere (C. W. Anderson, 2011b; Domingo et al., 2015), as well as looking at other actors than journalists within the newsroom (like tech developers, metrics analysts, and marketing personnel) (S. C. Lewis & Westlund, 2015a).

Second, doing ethnographic research about digital news production is almost impossible without access to key software, like content management systems and communication applications. Both authors of this book have experienced, when doing ethnographic fieldwork, the silence of modern newsrooms, a silence reflecting the digitisation of all communication in applications like Slack and other digital workspace communication and workflow tools. Without access to the tools in use, it is almost impossible to capture anything sensible about what's going on in the production process. Such access is as essential as "getting a newsroom identification badge that lets the researcher come and go as needed throughout the observation period" (Robinson & Metzler, 2016, p. 455). Other applications and technological and material artefacts might also be important, like actively following the involved journalists and others on social media or tracing which artefacts are important for the production process. However, the amount of digital communication data to be traced, captured, and included in the final analysis can be so overwhelming that it is an almost impossible task to undertake, simply because "too much is going on in digital spaces to truly be observed" (Robinson & Metzler, 2016, p. 456). Furthermore, capturing, storing, and analysing data from communication applications and other software and artefacts might involve ethical issues related to harvesting personal data that are difficult to address properly.

These difficulties aside, the production, distribution, and consumption of news in digital times is so complex and fast-changing that the insights brought forth by qualitative, ethnographic research is pivotal in order to get a sense of how digital journalism develops. A different aspect related to this is the ways in which audiences and news consumption has become intertwined with the practices of news making, an aspect we will turn to in the next section.

7.4 Audience research

A key characteristic of the digital news environment is that audiences have a magnitude of options to access news on the platforms and times of their own choosing in a "hybrid media system" (Chadwick, 2013), in which legacy and emerging media are intertwined. This, combined with the many ways in which audiences can participate in, contribute to, and even make their own news production and distribution systems, has spurred a wave of research interest in the ways in which audiences access, contribute to, and understand news and journalism. The "audience turn" (Costera Meijer, 2020) is also reflected in journalistic practice itself, as journalists, editors, and news companies have become increasingly pre-occupied with audience reach and engagement (e.g., Chua & Westlund, 2019; Ferrer-Conill & Tandoc, 2018; Nelson, 2018; see also chapter 3, section 3.3).

Consequently, the methods by which to study audiences and their interactions with news and journalism in digital times have become diversified. Classical methods like surveys, interviews, and focus groups have been accompanied by methods like Q methodology and a range of digital methods to measure audience engagement and interaction with news. Some of these methods are similar to the big data and computational network analysis methods discussed in the previous section, like for instance using software like CrowdTangle to analyse how audiences interact with news on Facebook and Instagram (e.g., Majo-Vazquez, Mukerjee, Neyazi, & Nielsen, 2019). Using such audience metrics for analysis of audience behaviour can, however, be compromised by "inherent reductionism" (Schrøder, 2016, p. 531) because audiences are being "reduced to quantifiable aggregates: herds of masses rather than creative individuals or groups" (Heikkilä & Ahva, 2015, p. 50).

However, the digital traces that audiences leave behind when interacting with news and journalism can also be analysed with more qualitative approaches, for instance those affiliated with "virtual ethnography", in which researchers trace digital discussion forums, comments, or other user-generated online material in order to get a sense of for instance how various groups of audiences discuss, make sense of, and/or interact with news (see for instance Bird & Barber, 2007). Such virtual ethnographies can be combined with computational methods that cast a wider net over audience interactions with news, as is illustrated by Steensen's (2018) analysis of the Norwegian Twitter sphere during a 2011 terrorist attack. Overall, mixed-method approaches to audience research are becoming more common, according to Schrøder (2016), who mentions Jensen and Sørensen's (2013) combination of surveys, focus groups, and virtual ethnographies in their analysis of Facebook users, and a Finnish research project applying various methods in tracing nine different groups of audiences' interaction with news and journalism over a period of one year (see Heikkilä & Ahva, 2015, where the methodology of this study is discussed).

Another method which has become popular is analysing media or news *repertoires*, a concept that reflects the patterns of media and news use which audiences establish over time (Peters & Schrøder, 2018). The advantage of such a methodological approach is that it takes spatiotemporal relations into account and acknowledges that the ways in which audiences interact with and relate to news are rooted in both habits established over time and socio-cultural contexts. One way of analysing news and media repertoires is to apply Q-methodology, which aims at tapping into audiences' subjective experiences with a specific "discursive universe" (for instance news) through exposing them to a set of cards containing statements about an aspect of the universe in question (Schrøder, 2016, p. 534). The participants then sort the cards according to which statements they agree and disagree with.

Adopting Q-methodology to the study of news use is an example of innovative methodological advancements in digital journalism studies. Such creative adaptations of methods can be found in a range of audience-centric digital journalism research, like for instance using mood boards to make sense of young peoples' relation to news, or using storytelling, painting, or even poetry-writing and Lego installations in order to make sense of how people really relate to news (Costera Meijer, 2016, p. 548).

7.5 Concluding remarks

The methods we have discussed in this chapter are not the only ones currently being tested in digital journalism studies. Not by far. A range of research approaches with origins in various disciplines is being adopted, or is likely to be adopted in the future. Examples include "digital forensics" (Garfinkel, 2012), a method to detect for instance the origin, validity, and reliability of digital content; "technography" (Kien, 2009) – ethnography of technology – suited to trace the workings and doings of technology in social contexts; and conversation analysis of audience interactions in online news spaces (Steensen, 2014). Experimental studies are also becoming increasingly popular, for instance to test whether audiences can spot the difference between robot- and human-produced news (see for instance Clerwall, 2014; Haim & Graefe, 2017; Waddell, 2018); to test how journalists respond to new software (Lindholm, Backholm, & Högväg, 2018); or to develop and test new technological applications related, for instance, to location-based journalism (Nyre, 2015; Nyre et al., 2012). These latter studies point to a new challenge related to studying news consumption. As news consumption has moved to mobile devices, it is difficult to assess how the context of news use affects how news is understood and consumed, simply because the context is constantly changing.

As we have discussed with big data methods in this chapter, there is a risk that new methods bear with them a fascination that goes way beyond what they actually can achieve. New methods can no doubt have that effect, just as new technologies and artefacts can have a blinding effect on the practitioners of journalism (Posetti, 2018). Digital journalism scholars should therefore remain sceptical concerning the new methods they apply and ask *what* this method can achieve that other methods cannot, and whether applying the new method will provide *new, valuable knowledge* that otherwise would have remained unknown.

The future of digital journalism studies will undoubtedly imply experiments with even more new methods, some of which will be adopted from other disciplines, and some, which someone yet has to invent and develop. What else the future might bring is the topic of the final chapter of this book.

8 The futures

Deconstructions of and directions for digital journalism studies

We began this book by referring to the Facebook CEO Mark Zuckerberg's appearance before the US Congress in April 2018 following the Cambridge Analytics scandal. Going full circle, let us now return to that hearing and reflect on one sentence that the chairman, Republican congressman Greg Walden, offered during his opening statement. After praising Zuckerberg for his success with Facebook and characterising him as "one of the era's greatest entrepreneurs", Walden paused for a moment and said: "I think it is time to ask whether Facebook may have moved too fast and broken too many things".

This statement, of course, referred to the Facebook motto "move fast and break things", originally articulated to inspire coders to keep on coding and not worry about the mistakes they made. Facebook abandoned the motto in 2014 after it had taken on a life of its own as a symbol of how the company, and other tech giants, had grown incredibly fast while disrupting entire industries and changing public spheres and people's everyday lives with what many perceived as minimal social and moral responsibility (Taplin, 2017). Indeed, they did move fast. And they broke things. The motto became an emblematic embodiment of Christensen's (1997) theory of disruptive innovation, while simultaneously becoming an articulation of a discourse that has had a deep impact on both the journalism sector and digital journalism studies scholarship.

This discourse is the discourse of deconstruction. It was originally identified by Ahva and Steensen (2017) in their analysis of the fourth wave of digital journalism scholarship that dominated the field halfway through the second decade of the millennium. It is not only a discourse dominating digital journalism studies but a discourse that serves as a typical example of how the three dimensions of the framework we introduced in chapter 2 are interlinked. These three dimensions – society, sector, and scholarship – are important to keep in mind when looking at the broader pictures of what digital journalism studies is. *Society* refers to global, national, and local changes that influence and interrelate with the (journalism) *sector*, which encompasses the role and developments of journalism in society as an institution and phenomenon, as well as practice, service, profession, and product. *Scholarship* refers to epistemic practices of producing knowledge, and this book has focused exclusively on digital journalism studies as a distinct and transformative field intersecting with journalism studies and several other fields.

The urge both to deconstruct (in practice) and to articulate a *need* to deconstruct or a *sense of deconstruction* (as discourse) is something which marks both the sector and the scholarship. Within the scholarship of digital journalism studies, the discourse of deconstruction implies that researchers are searching to deconstruct core concepts, like "journalists", "journalism", "news", and "news company", in order to redefine them. As Reese noted (2016, p. 3): "[U]nlike many other more settled fields, journalism research has been obsessed with the very definition of its core concept – what journalism is".

However, this urge within scholarship to deconstruct did not emerge within a vacuum. Scholars repeatedly seek legitimacy for their studies by making reference to the discourses of disruption and crisis which significantly have influenced the journalism sector in recent years, as we discussed in chapter 6, section 6.1.1. The journalism sector has geared significant efforts for building its platform presence, closely followed and studied by researchers. There has been a separation of news from journalism where news rituals increasingly have moved beyond the production, distribution, and consumption of journalism, and are now exercised by alternative news media (Holt et al., 2019), fake news sites (Robertson & Mourão, 2020), and platforms non-proprietary to the news media (Ekström & Westlund, 2019b). Over the last couple of years, more and more publishers have shifted their focus back towards their proprietary platforms, engaging in platform counterbalancing.

The urge to deconstruct doesn't stop at the sector. The symbolic status of the "move fast and break things" motto, and the feeling that certain, important things indeed have moved too fast and broken too many things, is a feeling belonging to the dimension of society at large. This feeling is a sign of how the discourses of deconstruction, disruption, innovation, and crisis go beyond the sector of journalism to include many aspects of society, from people's everyday lives to politics, culture, and a wide range of industries. This feeling is what makes the "digital" in digital journalism studies much more than just an emphasis on binary code, in quite the same way as the Facebook motto transformed from an original emphasis on practices of coding to a symbolic diagnoses of contemporary society.

Realising how such discourses connect scholarship with both the sector and society also makes it apparent that the discourses dominating the scholarship are rooted in *specific* societies, and thereby specific sectors within those societies. Not all societies, and not all sectors, are marked by a feeling of things moving too fast and breaking too many things. The discourses of deconstruction, disruption, innovation, and crisis are predominantly discourses of the journalism sector in Western democracies. There is a tendency within digital journalism studies to forget this and assume that these discourses are not discourses originating from within specific societies and their sectors, and instead view them not at all as discourses but as universal facts. Such misconceptions should be avoided, and the scholarship should be more aware of the normative assumptions rooted in these discourses, as we discussed in chapter 6. It is important to have the three dimensions, scholarship, sector, and society and how they are connected, both discursively and in practice, in mind when formulating research questions, collecting data, analysing the findings, and drawing conclusions.

In this final chapter we offer some conclusions and directions for future research which are all rooted in this need to scrutinise the connections between scholarship, sector, and society. Next we discuss how the scholarship of digital journalism studies relates to the sector of journalism, specifically if the scholarship should be *for* or *about* the journalism sector. Then we briefly summarise the key takeaways from the preceding chapters of this book. We conclude the book by taking the liberty of assessing what we normatively envision is most important in the road ahead and chart five key directions for the 2020s. These directions shape the last section of this chapter.

8.1 Digital journalism studies *for* or *about* the sector

One normative approach in digital journalism studies involves developing research and knowledge *about* the frontiers of the field. Digital journalism studies scholars typically engage in basic science for the academic field. Applied science has ambitions to develop knowledge about the frontiers of the field *for*, and potentially *with* representatives of the journalism sector. For example, researchers can experiment with emerging technologies and develop newswork routines for or with newsworkers. While there are exceptions where scholars engage in such research about journalism and news (e.g., Bygdås, Clegg, & Hagen, 2019), digital journalism studies oftentimes travels forward in the back currents of the journalism sector rather than actively participating in shaping its developments through action research and other forms of applied science in which scholars actively contribute to the (re)construction and development of digital journalism in the journalism sector. Moreover, researching the innovators in the journalism sector can result in digital journalism studies scholars indeed contributing to building important knowledge that later adopters as well as journalism educators can get worthwhile guidance from. We do not suggest that digital journalism studies scholars exert no influence on the developments of the journalism sector, as such research findings and outputs are used in educating newsworkers of the future, and sometimes also used for policy making, managerial decision-making as well as public outreach and broader societal informing. Numerous scholars have participated as experts in public inquiries relating to the journalism sector, as well as platform companies, telecom, and media regulation. Some scholars have presented or conducted research for industry associations such as World Association of Newspapers (WAN-IFRA) and the International News Media Association (INMA), as well as for UNESCO and the World Economic Forum. Digital journalism studies clearly has much relevance in such contexts, but it means that the research must be communicated in ways and via means that reach and appeal to such stakeholders. Examples of such include, but are not limited to, the Digital News Report series from the Reuters Institute for the Study of Journalism (and other reports in their series) in the UK, as well as reports by the Pew Research Centre in the US and other research centres. Such outward-facing reports, or reports written for industry associations, can devote attention to mapping current developments, and discussion of ongoing trends, the future, and implications for how managers and policy makers may solve some of the key problems. We certainly agree on the importance of such reports, which well can be associated with academic publications too (written before or after the report).

However, journal articles differ from such reports, imposed with requirements of academic rigor and making advancements in the field. Digital journalism studies as a field plays an important role in raising the level of abstraction and analysis in research, which can help to guide scholars as well as practitioners and students seeking to explore and push the frontiers. Altogether, we think there is room for improvement across digital journalism studies in terms of interdisciplinary approaches, accumulation of knowledge, and development of theory and concepts. This does not mean that digital journalism studies should be mostly *about* the journalism sector. First, it should be sensitive to the societies *beyond* the sector and the relations between the sector and the society. Second, experimental research, applied research, and action research with or without sector cooperation should strive to build on and further develop theoretical dimensions in order to reach academic rigor and value to both the academic community and the sector. Third, making (theoretical) advancements to the academic field does not mean being irrelevant to the sector. In sectors, scholarships and societies influenced by discourses of deconstruction, disruption, innovation, and crisis, scholarship is not the only dimension in which theoretical discussions are relevant. Having a dialogue about how to deconstruct and redefine core concepts is relevant to both scholarship and the sector.

8.2 Key takeaways: the formative formations of the field

This book has offered a multidimensional analysis of the formation of digital journalism studies since the turn of the new millennium. Chapter 1 briefly charted the course for the entire book and highlighted how the Facebook Cambridge Analytica scandal illuminated key questions and debates about what a media company is. Digital journalism studies is ideally global but continues to have a European/North American dominance. The chapter introduced our meta-analysis of publications in the journal *Digital Journalism* from 2013 to 2019, which we throughout this book have used as an empirical basis to chart the field. The publications in this journal, however, do not constitute the whole field of digital journalism studies. There are many other publications (in other journals, in books, reports, and so on) that have contributed greatly to its formation. Nevertheless, we find that the journal *Digital Journalism* has played a significant role in shaping digital journalism studies, and that an analysis of this journal provides valuable insights into what the field looks like and how it has developed.

Based on this meta-analysis, we concluded in chapter 1 that digital journalism studies is an interdisciplinary field, but with a strong footing in sociology and communication. The field focuses on journalism and digital media yet is marked by having to consider a form of separation (or dislocation) of news from journalism as a key transition and premise. The introductory chapter outlined four key premises: 1) a massive shift in revenue streams because advertisers have largely migrated to the platform companies, and publishers have developed subscription revenues; 2) an increased emphasis on audience metrics and analytics in the journalism sector; 3) shifting patterns of distribution in which platform companies non-proprietary to institutions of journalism have gained dominance; and 4) journalism has become more vulnerable to manipulation, disinformation, and a consequent lack of public trust.

Chapter 2 explored current debates on how to define both digital journalism and digital journalism studies. Digital journalism is a phenomenon and practice of selecting, interpreting, editing, and distributing news about public affairs; it is linked to digital technologies and has a symbiotic relationship with its audiences. It is clearly interrelated with digital journalism studies as a field. Echoing Eldridge and colleagues (2019, p. 393), we argue it is important to see digital journalism studies as an interdisciplinary field in its own right, rather than as a sub-field of journalism studies that could reinforce a journalism-centric approach rather than the broader interplay between news, digitisation, and diverse actors in society. However, digital journalism studies scholars have covered some objects of inquiry much more thoroughly than others, which raises questions about what mechanisms are at play. This chapter introduced an analytical framework to analyse the dynamic and mutual relationship between the academic field and its object of inquiry, a framework consisting of the dimensions society, sector, and scholarship. The chapter further made a contribution by linking these dimensions to four key mechanisms that help advance knowledge into why digital journalism studies scholars pay much more attention to some topics of inquiry than others. These mechanisms are: 1) Issue (in)visibility, 2) Pro-innovation bias, 3) Path dependency, and 4) Addressability.

Chapters 3 and 4 focused on the most dominant thematic clusters in the research published in *Digital Journalism* – technology and platforms. Chapter 3 featured a review of the technology-oriented research in digital journalism studies and unpacked three key areas: data journalism, analytics and metrics, and algorithms and automation. Each of these areas has been the subject of one or even two special issues in the journal *Digital Journalism*, and they have become more distinct from each other over time. Moreover, the research in these areas connects with audiences, the third largest thematic cluster. Few digital journalism studies scholars have studied technology (as technological actants) per se, nor are there many that have integrated the study of actors with (technological) actants or audiences.

Chapter 4 focused on the second most dominant thematic cluster: platforms. We differentiated between platforms (like social media and search engines) and digital devices (desktop, smartphones, tablets, and others). The chapter introduced a wealth of research into platforms, which mostly has involved the study of social media platforms in Western contexts. Even though Facebook and WhatsApp are both attracting more users than Twitter, scholars have more often developed research designs involving the microblogging service. Few have studied Google, and few have studied Weibo, WeChat, Telegram, and other platforms mostly used in Asia and the global south. Much research has been marked by exploring how news publishers build a platform presence, and how citizens access and engage with the news in such ways. Relatively few albeit more and more scholars have approached these developments in a more critical way in the salient case of journalism, acknowledging that more is not necessarily better and that even platform counterbalancing may be necessary. To continue, the chapter showed that few scholars have used research designs for news production where they differentiate between desktop, smartphones, and other devices, although mobile has quickly displaced desktop as the main gateway for accessing the news.

Chapter 5 was devoted to the role of theory in digital journalism studies. It discussed a range of different theories adopted and used and what roles theory plays. Digital journalism studies draws upon theories from a wide array of fields and disciplines, and scholars are willing to experiment with new theoretical framings, especially from science and technology studies. However, there is a degree of path-dependency related to adoptions of theoretical frameworks common in journalism studies, mostly related to sociological and political science perspectives. Perspectives from the humanities (especially cultural and language studies) are lacking, implying that the languages, discourses, and sense-making mechanisms of digital journalism are under-researched, at least in the research published in *Digital Journalism*.

Chapter 6 focused on normativity in digital journalism. Digital journalism scholarship has been, and still is, often normatively framed within a discourse of crises or a discourse of technological optimism. This normativity is often hidden or taken-for-granted, in statements like "journalism is in crises" or "technology has much to offer journalism", which build on assumptions of external influences or opportunities affecting journalism and oftentimes fail to recognise the agency of journalism and its practitioners. We agree with those who argue that such assumptions should be avoided, and that scholars should develop a greater sensitivity towards, and transparency about, normativity (Althaus, 2012; Carlson et al., 2018). Moreover, a pro-innovation bias dominates the field, promoted by the discourse of change and innovation so salient in both the sector and scholarship. This bias can make research blind to the things that do not change, while at the same time overestimating the things that do change. However, we do not argue that all normativity should be avoided. In fact, we think scholars should think more carefully about in what respects the field of digital journalism studies *should* be normative. We think it is about time that scholars dare to approach questions related to digital journalism's societal role in more normative fashions, related, for instance, to how digital journalism can contribute to counter disinformation, political polarisation, and other processes of de-democratisation, and how digital journalism can contribute to solve problems like climate change and pandemics.

Chapter 7 explored the wealth of methods used in digital journalism studies, which includes some methods originating from information science and computer science. Digital journalism studies pays some attention to advancing content analysis with computational methods. Opportunities in how to accumulate and analyse data are explored not only for content analysis, but also for network analysis reflecting the increasingly networked nature of news distribution and consumption. We welcome such advancements, but also raise concerns about the risk of putting too much emphasis on the possibilities offered by emerging technologies and the availability of data instead of focusing on what the important research questions are. The chapter also discussed challenges and advancements in audiences-centric digital journalism scholarship and in ethnographic approaches.

Altogether, these chapters have offered multiple perspectives on the formation of digital journalism studies throughout the first two decades of the 21st century. In the final section of this concluding chapter we turn to our own normative directions for how we think the field of digital journalism studies should evolve in the 2020s.

8.3 Directions for digital journalism studies for the 2020s

Digital journalism studies covers a rapidly growing body of literature published in many different scientific venues. In this book we have mostly drawn on original articles published in *Digital Journalism* (from 2013 to 2019), and especially so in chapters 3 and 4. While our referencing may appear to deliver bibliographical richness, it nevertheless represents only a minor part of the enormous body of literature produced in the field. There are numerous journalism-focused journals, and there are many more journals welcoming submissions focusing on journalism and/or news. The 2010s ended with two encyclopedias that each generated hundreds of entries, and additionally we find several handbooks and book series. Ultimately, scholars in the field produce great amounts of research every year. Journalism Research News is a Finnish initiative that monitors and briefly introduces new research about journalism. As of the end of 2019 it monitored 118 journals in addition to books published by recognised publishers, and found more than 1100 relevant publications to journalism studies in 2019 alone. Turning to January 2020, Journalism Research News had listed 110 publications, essentially meaning an average of five new publications in journalism studies every workday of the week.

As discussed, digital journalism studies is interdisciplinary. Thus, scholars may have to navigate far larger research volumes. On the one hand, advancements of new research and knowledge should be welcomed and cherished, but ongoing expansions of the field also make it an increasingly difficult scholarly terrain to navigate. This book has shown that scholars have mobilised around several different thematic clusters, but even when it comes to the most dominant ones, there is much fragmentation. Scholars oftentimes define narrow boundaries for their articles, resulting in explicit advancements made being relatively minor.

In this section we take the liberty of assessing what we normatively envision is most important in the road ahead for digital journalism studies as a scholarly field. We focus our approach in this narrower way with the intention to advance the field, while we continue to acknowledge that scholars can contribute substantially to the development of the journalism sector and society. We write this as digital journalism studies scholars, and our views can diverge from those of other scholars, but also in comparison to media managers and news workers in the journalism sector.

One of our normative points of departure connects with this introductory discussion, and how digital journalism studies scholars, editors, and publishers potentially can reconsider their approaches to research and publishing in the 2020s. A second normative point of departure reconnects with our analytical framework proposed in chapter 2, with which we think it is important for digital journalism studies scholars to stay tuned to the ongoing developments of society and the journalism sector. Scholars should account for ongoing changes in the journalism sector so they can develop timely and important studies while maintaining a critical perspective. This may sound self-evident, but all too often we are exposed to research where scholars have stood on the shoulders of previous studies in developing their research designs, seeking to replicate, follow up, or add new geographical dimension, while having completely missed that the journalism sector has chosen or been forced to move on. Next, we chart a call involving a total of five directions: two directions for where digital journalism studies should slow down, and three directions where scholars need to step up.

1   Slowing down and improving overall research activity

Digital journalism studies is a highly influential and productive field, which generates a large number of publications every year. Many scholars are embedded in neo-liberal university environments, which mean that they are influenced by the so-called "publish or perish" dogma, encouraging (even expecting) scholars to produce a high number of publications. Younger scholars without tenure are especially exposed to such expectations and are benchmarked against each other when applying for jobs and when going up for tenure.

Quality, originality, and impact are of course important indicators, but we cannot look away from the fact that scholars are often evaluated based on the number of articles they produce for high-ranking journals. Individual scholars who do not fall into line essentially reduce their chances of a successful career. The downside of this may be that scholars slice and dice data for maximum output rather than method triangulation and presenting a holistic account of their work. This is a structural problem where publishers and the editors of journals and book series, as well as universities must take responsibility. Such actors can contribute to change in digital journalism studies, albeit this field is just one tiny fish in the sea.

We hereby encourage scholars to slow down their overall research output and change their mindset from maximising the total number of publications to maximising the depth and breadth of each of their publications. Journal articles should clearly advance the accumulation of knowledge in the field, something which can be done in multiple ways, including but not limited to theory-, concept- or method-development, synthesis, as well original empirical studies. Clearly word count restrictions are an important factor here, and in the world of online publishing journals can reconsider word count restrictions to allow high-quality works where more exhaustive reviews are in place, and where authors can present mixed methods and materials in a satisfactory way rather than having to split their studies into several publications.

We also encourage publishers not to push for establishing more journals and increasing the number of issues of established journals as submissions increase. There is also a tendency that publishers are driven by market interests and a striving to achieve competitive advantage instead of quality and originality in outputs, resulting in many similar publications, like for instance competing encyclopedias and handbooks. Finally, we encourage universities to pay more attention to quality and originality instead of quantity when assessing academic job applications and tenure promotions.

2 **Reducing data-driven research outputs**

The emphasis on API-based research (Venturini & Rogers, 2019), associated with collecting and analysing trace data as well as so-called big data, bring specific views on how knowledge is best acquired and what types of knowledge are needed to find the right answers to the questions asked by digital journalism researchers. We argue there is a risk that the availability of new types of data is increasingly setting the agenda for research questions and not the other way around. This creates a situation in which advancements of knowledge are created because there is available data, and not necessarily because there are new, important, and theory-driven questions that need to be answered. We certainly subscribe to the view that scholars in the field should analyse existing datasets when possible from a research point of view, and when this can advance theory and the field. However, too often scholars use industry data or cross-sectional surveys using measures that are not linked to theories or models. Repeatedly, scholars also carry out studies of their students, who constitute a very specific group, and thus should be avoided unless the study asks research questions focusing on student-specific experiences and populations per se, and when studying causal mechanisms in that specific group. It does little good to produce such articles with extensive discussions of findings and a short disclaimer about limitations in the end. Scholars need to refrain from conducting research with need for such disclaimers altogether.

Moreover, chapter 7 on methods showed that a substantial body of scholarship employs rather traditional methods, and often only one method. Clearly, there are constraints in word count to the standard journal article format, which understandably leads scholars to prioritise one method per publication. This calls for more flexibility from the perspective of journals, accommodating more word count for multi-method submission. This would correspond well with social scientists in digital journalism studies, who have long since argued that one should strive for method triangulation in research designs, something that enables richer and more diverse understandings of blind spots in the field and of evolving phenomenon in the journalism sector. At the same time, it should be noted that many scholars guided by approaches from the humanities and cultural studies resist the very idea of method triangulation and argue for the value of deep knowledge produced by using one qualitative method. We agree with this and argue that both deep analysis of specific aspects of digital journalism and broad knowledge produced by triangulation are necessary. All in all, we call for more theory-driven research in the 2020s, hoping to counterbalance the rise of data-driven research. We also hope that scholars from the humanities and cultural studies will advance their positions throughout the 2020s, contributing with theoretically informed research.

3 **A more nuanced understanding of the journalism sector**

Our chapters 3 and 4 focused exclusively on objects of inquiry and gave a glimpse into research produced across the two most dominant thematic clusters of the *Digital Journalism* journal throughout the 2010s: technology and platforms. The analytical framework helps surface instances where there is a disconnect between what is happening in the journalism sector and subsequent scholarship. The international reputation of specific news publishers, such as *The New York Times*, *The Washington Post*, and the *Guardian*, has resulted in a great number of studies into these particular companies. At the same time there is very little research into what Japanese and Indian news publishers of comparable size and readership do, and also less research into the local and regional news publishers that often form the backbone of journalism. Repetitive studies into some case studies means others are largely overlooked.

In this context, Deuze and Witschge (2020) stress that much research and field formation into the study of journalism has limited itself to the study of what institutional news publishers do, what they publish, and how such news material is accessed, while largely overlooking journalism by individuals and start-ups. We argue that journalism researchers should consider the porous borders of journalism and cannot study only what has formerly been seen as its centre. We must also study peripheral actors (see special issue by Belair-Gagnon et al., 2019) and alternative news media (Holt et al., 2019) in addition to other actors beyond the traditional news institutions in the Western world to understand journalism and related developments. Despite being a field generating enormous amounts of research there are clearly many relatively under-researched areas. Scholars have adopted pro-innovation biases and studied how journalists and news publishers appropriate and normalise practices with social media platforms such as Twitter into their work, and for personal branding. Fewer have studied and critically assessed the downsides of such ventures, when they become highly dependent on platform companies to function. Dependence on external parties to achieve organisational and utilitarian goals boils down to matters of power, and how journalists and publishers have become more dependent on platform companies for distribution, exposure, and engagement. Loss of advertising revenues means they have become more directly dependent on their audiences to function.

Moreover, the journalism sector has not communicated widely about developments of tools and systems designed for digital safety. Consequently, there is relatively little research into the intersection of journalism and digital safety, a fundamental component for journalists to continue their work in the 2020s. Moreover, there is a wealth of research into journalism, news, and politics where political elections are studied extensively and repeatedly. There is less attention paid to other realms and issues of politics, such as climate change and its consequences, and there is less attention paid to genres beyond political news. Research should pay more attention to different epistemologies of digital journalism (Ekström, Lewis, & Westlund, 2020; Ekström & Westlund, 2019a; Matheson & Wahl-Jorgensen, 2020), for instance how other genres, formats, and beats develop, like those associated with entertainment, leisure, human interest, sports, culture, and consumerism, to name but a few.

4   **Towards more diversity**

Much research in digital journalism studies and communication altogether, is dominated by Western perspectives and studies, especially by scholars in the US and Western/Northern Europe. Towards the end of the 2010s there was more and more debate into diversity among (digital) journalism scholars. Scholars across the globe need to speak to each other, bringing their very best scholarship to the forefront. There is a need for better positioning of research, and it does not make sense to continue traditions where the US is used as the benchmark, directly or indirectly. Clearly there is also a need for a more diverse composition of research published, including studies from all across the globe. This book shows that digital journalism studies, in the more specific context of research published in *Digital Journalism* (2013–2019), has a very strong Western bias: most articles published in the journal are authored by scholars based in the US and Western Europe. Some of these scholars originally come from the global south, or alternatively are based in the West and study digital journalism in the global south. Ultimately though, Western perspectives dominate theories, normative assumptions, methods, and geographical areas being studied. In 2019 there were more and more calls for, and conversations about, diversity in the field (Hess, Eldridge, Tandoc, & Westlund, 2019; Mutsvairo, 2019; Rao, 2019; Wright, Zamith, & Bebawi, 2019). Journalism journals have transformed the composition of their editorial boards to improve the diversity of voices and expertise across gender, geographies, methods, and so forth. The academic output is only one side of the coin. The other side essentially requires a rise in relevant and rigorous submissions from the global south than can succeed in peer-review processes and stimulate growth in number of published works from the global south.

5   **Improving accumulation of knowledge**

Research reviews are seldom sharp enough to be systematic and holistic. Instead, they are at times anecdotal, essentially helping the author(s) in arguing for their specific study. There are always several factors one can claim in relation to assertions, such as that no other scholar has previously studied factor X or Y, and in this country or with that method. However, absence of research does not necessarily mean that such research would be worthwhile. On the contrary, there may well be good reasons scholars have not researched the topic in question. As discussed, there are also herd behaviours resulting in many scholars following suit into the study of specific objects of study. With rather narrow yet sweeping literature reviews, oftentimes reproducing citations to a more limited number of authoritative scholars in the field, contributors are trying to gain legitimacy for their work. Some scholars are hardly ever cited despite having produced worthwhile original work. This has to do with issues such as Western dominance, as well as limitations in expertise about more diverse literature as well as constraints in word count. Pointing back to the introduction to this section, and our argument for reducing research output, authors, reviewers, and editors must become more observant about saturation and level of contribution, doing what they can to reduce the field from being flooded with articles that actually accomplish very little by way of advancing research. Research should stand on the shoulders of others, taking previous research findings into consideration, as they seek to advance new knowledge. As digital journalism studies enters the 2020s there is opportunity for the scholars in the field to develop more holistic and systematic approaches in their research reviews and research designs.

These five directions constitute our normative and critical assessment of what the future of digital journalism studies should hold (alongside more common held ground such as interdisciplinary research). This assessment, and other normative and critical assessments we have made throughout this book, are of course marked by who we are, where we stand, and where we come from. We are two white males from the Western world, with tenured positions as full professors at one of the largest universities in Norway. We move in the same academic circles and attend the same conferences. Moreover, we hold editorial roles for the journals *Digital Journalism* and *Journalism Practice*, which both have contributed significantly to the advancement of digital journalism studies. Our normative values and our academic standards feed into what is published, alongside what works are actually submitted and how reviewers assess them.

In recognition of this, we would like to end this book by saluting the diversity of digital journalism studies and encourage it even further. In a time when both digital journalism and digital journalism studies are marked by a discourse of deconstruction, implying that much about journalism previously taken for granted (like who is a journalist, where

Selected references

We list below a few key references mentioned in the preceding text. For the full bibliography of this book, please visit the online eResource at www.routledge.com/9780367200909.

Ahva, L., & Steensen, S. (2017). Deconstructing digital journalism studies. In S. A. Eldridge II & B. Franklin (Eds.), *The Routledge companion to digital journalism studies*. London and New York: Routledge.

Al-Rawi, A. (2019). Viral news on social media. *Digital Journalism*, 7(1), 63–79. https://doi.org/10.1080/21670811.2017.1387062

Bechmann, A., & Nielbo, K. L. (2018). Are we exposed to the same "News" in the news feed? An empirical analysis of filter bubbles as information similarity for Danish Facebook users. *Digital Journalism*, 6(8), 990–1002. https://doi.org/10.1080/21670811.2018.1510741

Belair-Gagnon, V., & Holton, A. E. (2018). Boundary work, interloper media, and analytics in newsrooms. *Digital Journalism*, 6(4), 492–508. https://doi.org/10.1080/21670811.2018.1445001

Boczkowski, P. J. (2004). *Digitizing the news: Innovation in online newspapers*. Cambridge, MA: MIT Press.

Boczkowski, P. J. (2010). *News at work: Imitation in an age of information abundance*. Chicago: University of Chicago Press. Retrieved from http://files/5332/books.html

Burgess, J., & Hurcombe, E. (2019). Digital journalism as symptom, response, and agent of change in the platformed media environment. *Digital Journalism*, 7(3), 359–367. https://doi.org/10.1080/21670811.2018.1556313

Bygdås, A. L., Clegg, S., & Hagen, A. L. (Eds.). (2019). *Media management and digital transformation*. Oxon, UK and New York: Routledge.

Carlson, M. (2018a). Confronting measurable journalism. *Digital Journalism*, 6(4), 406–417. https://doi.org/10.1080/21670811.2018.1445003

Carlson, M., Robinson, S., Lewis, S. C., & Berkowitz, D. A. (2018). Journalism studies and its core commitments: The making of a communication field. *Journal of Communication*, 68(1), 6–25. https://doi.org/10.1093/joc/jqx006

Chua, S., & Westlund, O. (2019). Audience-centric engagement, collaboration culture and platform counterbalancing: A longitudinal study of ongoing sensemaking of emerging technologies. *Media and Communication*, 7(1), 153. https://doi.org/10.17645/mac.v7i1.1760

Coddington, M. (2015). Clarifying journalism's quantitative turn. *Digital Journalism*, *3*(3), 331–348. https://doi.org/10.1080/21670811.2014.976400

Deuze, M., & Witschge, T. (2020). *Beyond journalism*. Cambridge, UK and Medford, MA: Polity Press.

Diakopoulos, N. (2015). Algorithmic accountability. *Digital Journalism*, *3*(3), 398–415. https://doi.org/10.1080/21670811.2014.976411

Domingo, D., & Paterson, C. (Eds.). (2011). *Making online news (volume 2). Newsroom ethnographies in the second decade of internet journalism*. New York: Peter Lang.

Ekström, M., & Westlund, O. (2019b). The dislocation of news journalism: A conceptual framework for the study of epistemologies of digital journalism. *Media and Communication*, *7*(1), 259–270. https://doi.org/10.17645/mac.v7i1.1763

Eldridge II, S. A., & Franklin, B. (Eds.). (2019). *The Routledge handbook of developments in digital journalism studies*. London: Routledge. https://doi.org/10.4324/9781315270449

Eldridge II, S. A., Hess, K., Tandoc, E. C., & Westlund, O. (2019). Navigating the scholarly Terrain: Introducing the digital journalism studies compass. *Digital Journalism*, *7*(3), 386–403. https://doi.org/10.1080/21670811.2019.1599724

Franklin, B., & Eldridge II, S. A. (Eds.). (2017). *The Routledge companion to digital journalism studies*. Oxon and New York: Routledge.

Helberger, N. (2019). On the democratic role of news recommenders. *Digital Journalism*, 1–20. https://doi.org/10.1080/21670811.2019.1623700

Hermida, A. (2010). Twittering the news. *Journalism Practice*, *4*(3), 297–308. https://doi.org/10.1080/17512781003640703

Lewis, S. C., & Molyneux, L. (2018). A decade of research on social media and journalism: Assumptions, blind spots, and a way forward. *Media and Communication*, *6*(4), 11. https://doi.org/10.17645/mac.v6i4.1562

Lewis, S. C., & Westlund, O. (2015a). Actors, actants, audiences, and activities in cross-media news work. *Digital Journalism*, *3*(1), 19–37. https://doi.org/10.1080/21670811.2014.927986

Moyo, D., Mare, A., & Matsilele, T. (2019). Analytics-driven journalism? Editorial metrics and the reconfiguration of online news production practices in African newsrooms". *Digital Journalism*, *7*(4), 490–506. https://doi.org/10.1080/21670811.2018.1533788

Paterson, C., & Domingo, D. (Eds.). (2008). *Making online news. The ethnography of new media production*. New York: Peter Lang.

Peters, C., & Broersma, M. (Eds.). (2013). *Rethinking journalism. Trust and participation in a transformed news landscape*. London: Routledge.

Peters, C., & Carlson, M. (2019). Conceptualizing change in journalism studies: Why change at all? *Journalism*, *20*(5), 637–641. https://doi.org/10.1177/1464884918760674

Singer, J. B., Hermida, A., Domingo, D., Heinonen, A., Paulussen, S., Quandt, T., . . . Vujnovic, M. (2011). *Participatory journalism. Guarding open gates at online newspapers*. Oxford, UK: Wiley-Blackwell.

Steensen, S. (2011). Online journalism and the promises of new technology. *Journalism Studies*, *12*(3), 311–327. https://doi.org/10.1080/1461670X.2010.501151

Steensen, S., Grøndahl Larsen, A. M., Hågvar, Y. B., & Fonn, B. K. (2019). What does digital journalism studies look like? *Digital Journalism*, 7(3), 320–342. https:// doi.org/10.1080/21670811.2019.1581071

Storsul, T., & Krumsvik, A. H. (2013b). What is media Innovation? In T. Storsul & A. H. Krumsvik (Eds.), *Media Innovations. A Multidiciplinary Study of Change* (pp. 13–26). Gothenburg: Nordicom.

Tandoc, E. C. (2019a). *Analyzing analytics. Disrupting journalism one click at a time.* London: Routledge.

Usher, N. (2016). *Interactive journalism: Hackers, data, and code.* Urbana: University of Illinois Press.

Waisbord, S. (2019). The 5Ws and 1H of digital journalism. *Digital Journalism*, 7(3), 351–358. https://doi.org/10.1080/21670811.2018.1545592

Witschge, T., Anderson, C. W., Domingo, D., & Hermida, A. (Eds.). (2016a). *The SAGE handbook of digital journalism.* London, Thousand Oaks and New Delhi: Sage.

Zamith, R. (2018). Quantified audiences in news production. *Digital Journalism*, 6(4), 418–435. https://doi.org/10.1080/21670811.2018.1444999

Zelizer, B. (2019a). Why journalism is about more than digital technology. *Digital Journalism*, 7(3), 343–350. https://doi.org/10.1080/21670811.2019.1571932

Index

Note: Page numbers in *italics* indicate a figure and page numbers in **bold** indicate a table on the corresponding page.

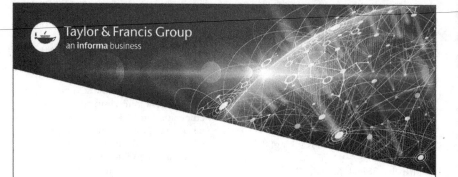